Time Matters
Making the Most of Your Day

Julia Rowan

MANAGEMENT
BRIEFS

Essential Insights for Busy Managers

Acknowledgements

My father, Fergus Rowan, knew what was important in life. My mother, Kathleen Rowan, is inspirational and resourceful.

Thanks to my sisters Anna, Sophie, Amy and Eve, to Eileen Fitzgerald, Eimear Gallagher, Alan McNeilly, Chris McNeilly, Fiona Murdoch, Eimear O'Broin and Karen O'Donnell, for valuable feedback. My brothers, Francis, Michael, Paul, John and Danny support me in so many ways.

For Anthony, who knows that there is so much more to life than watching the clock. And Paul, Tom and Catherine with whom all the time in the world would not be enough.

Julia Rowan

November 2009

© 2009 Julia Rowan
ISBN 1-906946-04-3
ISBN 978-1-906946-04-3

All design, art work and liaison with printers has been undertaken by
Neworld Associates, 9 Greenmount Avenue, Harold's Cross, Dublin 12. www.neworld.com

Publisher: Managements Briefs, 30 The Palms, Clonskeagh, Dublin 14.

Table of Contents

Forward

Julia Rowan has written this book in an easy-to-read style with plenty of tips for maximising your time management.

It is a very welcome addition to our developing series of Human Resource, Organisation Behaviour and General Management Books.

All books in the series aim to capture the essentials for busy managers; essential knowledge and skills are presented in an accessible easy-to-read style.

A list of books already published within the series appears on the on the final page of the book; our website www.ManagementBriefs.com lists forthcoming titles.

You the reader are very important to us and we would welcome any contact from you; it will only improve our products and our connection to our reader population.

Frank Scott-Lennon
Series Editor
frank@ManagementBriefs.com

November 2009

Introduction and Getting Started

Introduction and Getting Started

→ So many tasks, so little time...

→ No one pays you to manage your time

→ The simplicity of good time management

→ Making the most of this book

→ Exercises — do now, use later

→ Case Studies

How often do you have the kind of day where you work hard but go home with the feeling that you have achieved little? Do you have enough thinking time? Are you too busy to keep up with developments in your profession or sector? Does everything at work seem urgent? Are you enjoying your job as much as you would like?

Despite legislation which protects us and technology designed to help us become more effective, employees nowadays spend longer at work, feel more overwhelmed by the amount of work they have to do and have become more stressed. As organisations struggle to remain competitive, employees must find ways to manage their own personal effectiveness; getting a good job done while taking care of their health and wellbeing.

No one pays you to manage your time

Lets take a harsh view: Managing your time is not your job. Nobody pays you to do it. When you are praised or even promoted at work, it will not be because you have operated a good time management system. Going for a job interview, you may make, at most, a passing reference to your time management skills, but you will more likely focus on 'real' achievements, like reducing costs, completing important projects and increasing the customer base.

Your time management is like the operating software on your computer. It runs in the background, enabling you to achieve more in less time and to enjoy your challenges at work. Whether you work for yourself, for government, in industry or providing a service, the better you manage your time, the more successful you will be.

The simplicity of good time management

People who manage their time well do three essential things:

→ They make good decisions about what is important

→ They develop habits which enable them to follow-through on these decisions

→ They manage their environment

More than anything else, managing time is about managing choice. There is always too much to do and you have to decide on what to spend:

→ **more time** – when time spent will add long-lasting value, e.g. developing strategy, creating infrastructure, expanding the client base

→ **enough time** – when time spent means a good-enough job, e.g. preparing internal presentations and reports

→ **less time** – when time spent keeps things ticking over but does not add value, e.g. ensuring compliance, administration

→ **no time** – when not to get involved, e.g. responding to organisation-wide email or chasing rumours

The good news is that you have much more choice than you think. The bad news is that, like most people, you may have developed habits which prevent you from exercising this!

Every action you take is based on choice. Each time you access your email, answer the phone or pick up a file, you have chosen to react to a stimulus. So becoming aware of your choices (and then making good decisions) is a critical first step in managing your time.

Making the most of this book

There are a couple of points worth bearing in mind as you read through this book:

COST-BENEFIT: All of your time management decisions and practices have both costs and benefits. A manager who works with the door closed has privacy and more opportunity to concentrate, but may be perceived as aloof and miss what is going on. One who works with the door open will be connected to what is going on but is more likely to experience frequent interruptions. All of the suggestions in this book have costs and benefits and it is important to find what will work for you. Some

ideas will seem immediately useful. Others, not so. (But be aware that the ideas you most actively resist may be the ones worth looking at most closely!).

PLANNING: Planning can be as simple as taking five minutes to think and jot down ideas. When under pressure, it is hard to avoid plunging straight into action. But it is worth remembering why planning is such a great use of your time:

→ It means that you don't have to carry ideas in your head and enables you to concentrate on important issues.

→ It helps your memory. It is easier to remember something that you have thought about, written and seen, than something which you have only thought about. So even if you lose your plan, it was worth making it!

→ Once ideas are written down your sub-conscious brain starts to process them and you deliver better results.

You plan with a pencil. You do not carve your plans in stone with a hammer and chisel. You write them (on paper or screen) **based on the best current information.** If the context changes (or, more likely, as it changes) you adapt your plan. But having a plan is almost always better than not having one. Remember, planning is about focusing your attention - not predicting the future.

TECHNOLOGY: Technology can be a real help or a major hindrance. Most people value the fact that a document emailed from Australia can be printed in Europe 10 seconds later. Many people use software cleverly to help them manage their time. But remember that people construct their habits on the basis of the available technology. Originally copies of documents were laboriously hand-written. Carbon paper, photocopies and stencils speeded up copying. Air-mail, couriers and fax speeded up delivery times. Nowadays email transmits documents almost instantaneously. And this has changed people's expectations about response times.

TIME MANAGEMENT SYSTEM: Many time management courses and books focus on systems for managing your time, some quite complex. While the system you use matters, it is more important to make sure that you use good decision-making strategies. This book will help you to develop a time management system which follows the tried and tested scientific principles of economy, parsimony and simplicity. Remember, it is unlikely that anybody will ever ask to see your time management system and it will certainly not be audited!

Exercises — do now, use later

You probably want to start looking for solutions and ideas as soon as possible. But changing habits is much more difficult than learning new skills. By going through the exercises that follow, you will get a much clearer picture of how you are managing your time at the moment and will generate data that will help you make long-lasting changes.

Only one of the exercises takes time (the time log) but it is probably the most useful one to complete. All of the others take less than three minutes. Be as honest as you can when you are doing them.

Exercise 1 — time log

Most people find that keeping a time log gives them invaluable information about how they are spending their time. With a time log, you record everything you do over a couple of hours or even a day, including every interruption. (It is very important to record as you switch between tasks so that you capture all the details). It can become irritating to write down all the small tasks we do, including the interruptions. However the first step to changing ingrained habits is to see them clearly. Complete your time log on a sheet of paper or open a word document on your computer. Here is the information you need:

TIME	TASK – what you worked on	INTERRUPTION (emails, phone calls, callers, alarms)	COMMENTS
08.30			
08.45			
09.00			

Exercise 2 – my job

Reflect on what you are employed to do in your current job. Write down your key responsibilities/ tasks (3 to 5).

1

2

3

4

5

Exercise 3 — my first hour at work

Think carefully through your first hour at work. Typically, what do you do? Include as much detail as possible.

Exercise 4 — 'if only'

All of us have tasks that we would do 'if only' we had the time. Imagine that you do have the time; that every morning you walk into work knowing that all of your urgent work has been completed, and knowing that you will be able to work uninterrupted for one hour before turning to the day's normal tasks. If you had this hour at work every day, how would you spend it?

Case Studies

Managing your time better often requires a creative leap of imagination. The material in this book has been developed and tested at time management workshops for more than 10 years. I always ask workshop participants not to make up their minds immediately as to what will or will not work for them. Rather, to hold all ideas as 'potentially useful' at least for a while.

All of the short scenarios are true, although names and minor details have been changed. I have also included some unorthodox ways that workshop participants have shared with me as to how they get more out of their day. These are included, not as advice, but as a way of stimulating your own creativity as to how you can manage your time more effectively.

Summary of Introduction and Getting Started

→ People are working harder and longer and experiencing higher levels of stress

→ Technology has changed expectations about how urgent things are

→ Planning is crucial to delivering better results

→ All of your actions, and all of the changes that you will make, have both costs and benefits

→ When you pare time management back to its essentials, it is about managing choice

→ Your time management system should be as simple as possible.

9

Notes

Managing Your Attitude

1

Chapter outline
Managing Your Attitude

→ How your effectiveness starts with your thinking

→ What outcome do you want from this?

→ Which comes first, the thought or the behaviour?

→ Attention and Attitude — how you perceive things

→ Beliefs and Thoughts — how you make sense of things

→ Behaviour and Habits — how you do things

→ Getting your thinking straight — as simple as ABC...DE

How your effectiveness starts with your thinking

For sports people at the top of their game, it is not just their skills that differentiate them from their nearest rivals: it is mainly their attitude. How much they want success; how they can remain focussed and hold their nerve. In show-business, the willingness to push yourself can be more important than your ability to sing. In politics, the list of setbacks that Abraham Lincoln overcame before he went on to become US President is well-documented. In life, much of our success is down to our attitude. And for you, too, much of your success at work starts before you ever walk into your office, design a system, attend a meeting or make a proposal. Your attitude has a profound impact on your effectiveness at work.

And the problem is not just staying positive when faced with ever-increasing workloads: In many organisations a 'busy' culture has developed where employees engage in long conversations about how hard they are working, how much overtime they have done, and how many emails they receive every day. Activity, rather than productivity, receives a lot of attention and airtime and the employee who is leaving on time after working effectively all day can be greeted with "enjoy your half day" by colleagues who have spent much of the day tele-socialising, tipping in and out of small jobs and who are now settling down for a couple of hours overtime.

And for you, too, much of your success at work starts before you ever walk into your office, design a system, attend a meeting or make a proposal. Your attitude has a profound impact on your effectiveness at work.

It can be difficult to work in that culture — and difficult not to get sucked into those conversations about 'busyness'. My advice to anybody who finds those conversations going on is not to stop them — just change the subject if you can. Being a really good time manager does not automatically make you the most popular person on the team. But it's your time. You only get it once. And you want to make the most of it.

Some of the questions and thoughts on the following pages are designed to really get you thinking about your time because the more conscious you are about what you do and why you do it, the easier it will be for you to make changes.

What outcome do you want from this?

Have you picked up this book out of general interest, or do you have specific areas that you need help with? You will be more successful making changes if you can work out why you are not managing your time more effectively; also if you can clarify exactly what effective time management means to you.
Try this exercise:

Imagine that somebody important to you has been following you around for the past week with a video camera and they have handed you a very long tape! In terms of your time management, what would you see/hear on that tape that you are happy with? What would you see/hear on that tape that you are not happy with?

Now, imagine that in one month's time, that same person will spend another week recording your activity on a video camera, which you will then review. How will this tape be different? What will you see/hear on this tape that proves you are managing your time more effectively? What will you feel? What will you think? How will work be different?

Spend a little time reflecting, on the following questions:

→ How do you know that you have a time management problem? Be specific.

→ How will you know when you have fixed it?

→ What benefit do you derive from your current behaviour? (There is always a reason for doing something, even behaviour that is harmful, e.g. smoking). Finding the 'benefit' of your poor time management behaviours, can help you to overcome them.

→ When do you want to start managing your time better?

→ What will you gain by managing your time better?

→ What might get in the way of managing your time better? (Think about how you might get in your own way as well as obstacles that others may put in your way).

Which comes first, the thought or the behaviour?

Many people rightly believe that their behaviour (what they say and do) is caused by their attitude: "I smile because I feel happy". What they do not realise is that their behaviour can also change their thoughts and attitudes; put very simply "I feel happy because I smile". There is a feedback loop which encompasses how we perceive the world (our attention and attitude), how we make sense of the world (our beliefs and thoughts) and what we do in the world (our behaviour and habits).

Some people have a performance-enhancing loop: a positive attitude and can-do approach, thinking about options, talking about possibilities, getting on with the job and seeing the results. Others have a performance-inhibiting loop: a negative attitude, expecting failure, half-hearted performance and the consequent result confirming that indeed 'it doesn't work'.

Let's look at a few points on this loop:

Attention and Attitude – how you perceive things

Have you ever had the situation where you were considering buying a car and suddenly find that there are loads of them being driven around the streets? Did you ever sit in a library opposite someone who kept clearing their throat? After a while, you stopped reading and just sat there, anticipating the noise. Meanwhile, the person beside you was completely engrossed in their study and did not hear a thing!

While we may think that we perceive the world exactly as it is, each of us filters the information that is around us all the time. These filters are subconscious but very powerful. They determine:

→ What we notice – doesn't it seem that, when you are in a hurry, more of the traffic lights have turned red?

→ How we interpret information – "he said I look great today, that's nice!" or "he said I look great today, does that mean I normally look bad?"

→ What we remember – 'positive' people remember more nice things, 'negative' people remember more unpleasant things

There is an old saying 'where your attention goes, your energy flows'. It is worth becoming aware of what attracts your attention and reflecting on what may be happening that escapes your attention. We have problem-solving brains which means that we tend to notice what is wrong while very often good things pass by unnoticed. This can lead to a build-up of stress and a narrowing of the choices that we perceive.

Beliefs and Thoughts — how you make sense of things

Everybody has beliefs about themselves and others — what they are good at, what is 'OK', the type of person they are. Normally we are not conscious of our beliefs, they operate powerfully and silently in the background.

We often only notice them when we are faced with a situation that we find difficult. Somebody who has never led a team through a competitive tendering process is asked to spearhead a major proposal project. Their belief will determine whether they respond *"Yes. This is challenging but I'll do it"* or *"Oh no. This is going to be really difficult. I'm just not good at this kind of thing".*

Here are some ways to identify your beliefs:

→ Some beliefs are stereotypes, a kind of cognitive short-cut which prevents you having to do too much thinking. The stereotype can even be about yourself - "I always", "I never"

→ Beliefs are often the result of conditioning (either by yourself or others), and often come out as statements about the self - "I should", "I must", "I can't"

→ Beliefs emerge any time you feel uncomfortable or stressed about things - "I'm not that kind of person", "That's just who I am", "I can't make cold calls".

An expectation is another type of belief. We form expectations all the time but are often not aware of them until they are challenged. Have you ever spoken to somebody a number of times on the phone and then met them and found yourself thinking *'but you don't look like that!'*

Like beliefs, expectations drive behaviour in a powerful way. If you need to talk to somebody very senior in your organisation (or sector), you will probably expect to make an appointment a number of days, or even weeks, in advance, but if you need to meet a junior person, you would expect to see them quickly.

Behaviour and Habits — how you do things

The way we speak and act reflects our beliefs and thoughts. But the words we use also shape and reinforce our thoughts and beliefs. Saying 'I can't' often reflects an attitude rather than an ability. Saying 'I have to' is more likely to reflect a preference than an imperative.

While differences in wording may appear superficial, a growing body of research suggests that how we talk about things can change our experience.

And our actions can change our experience too. Think about what it looks like when you walk into work. Do you walk a little bit more

17

quickly as you reach your office, straighten your back and stride

In an experiment by Levins and Gaeth (1987) a group of people was asked to taste some food. Half of the group was told that the meat used in the food was 75% lean while the other half was told that the meat used was 25% fat. When asked to assess how tasty and healthy the food was, the '75% lean' group rated the meal healthier and tastier than the '25% fat' group. But all of the food came out of the same pot!

out? Or do you slow down, slouch a little, and take smaller steps? When picking up the phone to a 'difficult' customer or colleague, do you 'steel' yourself, roll your eyes to heaven and sigh or do you smile as you dial the number and ask for them with

a cheery voice? Your behaviour reinforces your feelings – and could quite possibly change them!

Think about how a really effective person behaves – how do they dress, walk, answer the phone? How do they organise themselves and interact with other people. What is their office space like?

In one-to-one coaching, coaches often advise clients to 'act as if', in other words, to take on the behaviour and see what difference that makes to how the client thinks and feels about an issue. If you were going to 'act as if' you were an excellent time manager, what would you see yourself doing, hear yourself saying? What changes would you make?

Whistle your way to work!

Another way in which attitudes become manifest is through our behaviour – but did you know that your behaviour can also shape your attitude?

In the song 'I whistle a happy tune' (from the film 'The King and I'), Anna, the Governess, tells her son:
"Whenever I feel afraid / I hold my head erect / And whistle a happy tune / So no one will

suspect / I'm afraid."

Later in the song, Anna shares the unintended consequences of this behaviour:
"The result of this deception / is very strange to tell / for when I fool the people I fear/ I fool myself as well

I whistle a happy tune / and every single time / the happiness in that tune / convinces me that I'm not afraid."

Getting your thinking straight — as simple as ABC...DE

Below is a powerful exercise devised by US Clinical Psychologist, Dr Albert Ellis, who suggests that it is not external events such as a delayed plane or broken computer that cause us stress. Rather it is our belief about those events that causes us stress. We sometimes see this in daily life when two people have completely different responses to the same event.

Either consciously or sub-consciously, stress is a choice. As with any choice, we can examine it to see whether it is useful. The stress response evolved with the single objective of priming our bodies to either run or fight. This was useful if you were faced with a hungry lion, but not so useful if you are stuck in an airport waiting for a plane that is delayed.

Ellis came up with the fantastic ABCDE exercise which can help us to get into the habit of recognising and correcting stress-inducing beliefs:

Activating Event	Your boss asks you to make a presentation
Belief - how you think about what's happened	"Oh no. I'm useless at making presentations. I'll probably dry up and I know that the Financial Controller will ask awkward questions."
Consequences – the result of your belief on your emotions and behaviour	Spend hours on the presentation Lose sleep Put every word on your slides – just in case
Dispute your belief	"They wouldn't have asked me if they didn't think I could do it. This is a chance for me to shine. There is a possibility that I'll dry up, so I'll prepare notes."
Effect of disputing the belief	Some self-belief creeps in The presentation seems do-able You might even enjoy it!

Summary of Chapter 1

→ If you want to build a good foundation for success, adopt a two-pronged approach. Start on the inside — with your attitudes, beliefs and thoughts — and on the outside — with your behaviour and language

→ On the inside: Start to notice some of the factors that drive your decisions about how you use your time. Pay attention to:

- Managing where your attention is going

- Altering negative thinking habits or patterns

→ On the outside: Start by

- Behaving 'as if' you were an effective time manager

- Using more positive verbal and body language that reflects the choices that you make about your time. Being more effective at work starts with a positive attitude, with believing that you have choices and being committed to making changes and achieving better results.

Managing Your Productivity

Chapter outline
Managing Your Productivity

→ 5 habits that might be holding you back
  - Being interrupted and getting distracted
  - Task switching
  - Using too many task reminders
  - Starting with the smaller tasks
  - Urgency addiction
→ Your two key hours at work and how to make the most of them

5 habits that might be holding you back

Something funny is happening: we are working longer hours and using more technology at work. But our productivity – the value we get from that time – is not increasing. German time management expert, Lothar Seiwert, estimates that the average person works at 40% productivity. This is mainly due to poor habits.

The reality for most people is that work is a very tiring place, physically and mentally. Work is also a cluttered place: desks piled high with papers, inboxes full of mails, messages and reminders coming from all angles. We work hard, often rushing around for the day before going home exhausted.

Habits are powerful. Good habits save (and poor habits waste) huge amounts of time and energy. This chapter highlights five key reasons why most people work hard without getting the return they deserve:

❶ Being interrupted and getting distracted

❷ Task switching

❸ Using too many task reminders

❹ Starting with the smaller tasks

❺ Urgency addiction

In this chapter, we are going to drill down and look at how you currently make decisions about how you use your time. Some suggestions are made to help you get more from your day. More suggestions follow in later chapters.

❶ **Being interrupted and getting distracted**

What Happens? You're working on something important, the phone rings and even though you let it go to voice mail, you have been interrupted. Then you are notified about an incoming email, even without looking at the email, you have been interrupted. In the workplace nowadays, we are interrupted, on average, once every nine minutes (more in open-plan offices, less in offices with closed doors) and the time between interruptions is decreasing.

Why is this a problem? When you are working on simple tasks, interruptions are generally not a problem, it is easy to get back on track. But they are a problem when you are working on something that needs your full attention, or when you have a tight deadline.

While your subconscious brain can handle tens of tasks at a time, your conscious brain can only focus on one thing. When you are interrupted your conscious brain switches to the interruption and then needs to switch back to the task on which you are trying to concentrate. This is time-consuming and tiring.

Your Issues

→ Use your time log to find who is interrupting you and why. What needs do the interruptions point to?

- People asking for information - a training need

- People asking to get documents signed or authorised because there is no set way of looking after this

- A discipline need - people not bothering to look up something themselves because asking you is easier

- An availability need - some of your job happens at unscheduled times

→ Reflect on whether it would make sense to set up a system to communicate on a regular basis with key people – your boss, direct reports, peers, key suppliers - and encourage them to do the same for you.

→ Set up a small file for each person and keep notes of delegated work, ongoing projects, ideas to discuss, items which require follow-up, in these files; so that when you are speaking to these key people you can catch up with a number of items at the same time.

→ Or organise a regular meeting time (daily or weekly) where all these issues are dealt with in one go.

2 Task switching

What happens? We constantly switch from one type of task to another. We do a couple of emails, then make a phone call, deliver a document, get a coffee, sign papers, do some work on a presentation and then check the inbox.

Why is this a problem? Constant switching of tasks means that there is a loss of focus and concentration. Economies of scale are not harnessed and consequently work takes longer. It can often lead to reacting to what is happening around you rather than pro-actively making decisions about what to do.

Your issues:

Think through your past few days at work and identify which of the following were reasons for moving from one task to another. Tick which apply to you.

- Doing a task that was on a list

- Doing a task because it was quicker than putting it on a list

- Responding to a new email, ringtone or reminder

- Working on something that you had noticed on your desk

- Doing a task before you forgot it

- Doing a task to meet a deadline

- Getting bored and moving on to a more interesting task

- Getting distracted, perhaps while surfing the net or looking through a file

- Following a normal routine (first I do task A, then task B)

- Making time for a task that was important but not urgent

- Switching to a task or spending extra time on it mainly because you like it

- Doing a task that you did not have time to delegate

- Doing small tasks as you didn't have enough time or energy to do important tasks

The chances are that you have ticked many of these reasons. For now, start to become more aware of what is driving your decision-making about moving from one task to another.

3 Using too many task reminders

What happens? Most people record the tasks they have to do in 10 different places.

Why is this a problem? Imagine 10 wardrobes with your clothes randomly distributed between them. It would be hard to decide what to wear. Similarly, when your tasks are stored in many different places, it is harder to make a quality decision about how to spend your time. Managing the lists becomes a task in itself and this can lead to less useful decision-making strategies.

We constantly switch from one type of task to another. We do a couple of emails, then make a phone call, deliver a document, get a coffee, sign papers, do some work on a presentation and then check the inbox.

Your Issues

Tick which task reminders you use.

- To-do list (written or electronic)
- Papers and files on the desk — waiting for your attention
- Email inbox — with un-actioned emails
- Mobile phone reminders/ text messages
- Computer reminders
- Computer calendar
- Paper or electronic diary
- Messages on post-its and other bits of paper
- Performance management form (or other documents which record your goals)
- Voicemail
- Instant-messaging, Real-time or other chat-room technology
- Memory
- Somebody to remind you (e.g. assistant)
- Other_____

  _____

  Total_____

We will come back to this, for now, make an effort to put all of your tasks onto one list.

④ Starting with the smaller tasks

If you have not already completed the exercises in the introduction, it would be useful to do exercises 3 and 4 on page 8 before you continue.

What happens? Most people spend their first hour at work on numerous quick, easy and fairly straightforward tasks which typically fall into four categories:

❶ Getting an overview of what the day holds, e.g., writing a to-do list, checking diaries and calendars

❷ Doing routine tasks, e.g., checking figures, making arrangements, completing paperwork

❸ Socialising/personal time, e.g., greeting colleagues, getting coffee, scanning the newspaper, checking bank accounts online

❹ Checking for potential problems, e.g., checking emails and listening to voicemails to see whether anything needs immediate attention

Why is this a problem? Often we do these small tasks with the best of intentions. We want to 'clear the decks' or get a few 'quick wins'. The problem is that most people fill their heads with large quantities of tasks first thing in the morning. This causes a feeling of stress and attention is paid to getting many small things off the list, often at the expense of the larger, more important tasks. Few of the tasks above would ever be discussed at a performance appraisal or promotion interview.

What is the alternative to starting with these types of tasks? When asked about tasks that they would love to have enough time for, most people identify five types of tasks:

❶ Thinking/planning — about a product, system, project, time-period

❷ Research — finding out what is going on in the organisation, industry, profession. Personal development

❸ People issues — working with team-members, consultation, coaching, delegation. Creating a network inside and outside the organisation. Getting close to customers

❹ Challenging projects — getting on with projects which are important, complex or have been put off

❺ Creating a robust infrastructure — creating systems, templates, procedures, policies which help you to get through your day-to-day work more quickly. Harnessing technology

We rarely pay enough attention to these tasks because they are not urgent. Yet, they would make a big difference to our work

Your Issues

Check to what extent the answers you gave to exercise 3 correspond to the four categories identified on page 26 and whether the answers you gave to exercise 4 correspond to the five categories above.

❺ **Urgency addiction**

<u>What happens?</u> Urgency addiction can happen at either a corporate or individual level. Urgent issues and long hours worked become high profile, attract attention and get talked about. Red exclamation marks become the norm on emails.

<u>Why is this a problem?</u> Urgency can be really useful. It can create a sense of energy and momentum that makes something important happen quickly.

Where urgency becomes a problem is when the organisation (or individual) starts to value activity over productivity. With a consequent loss of focus on what is really important.

Former President of the USA, General Dwight Eisenhower, said: "What is important is seldom urgent and what is urgent is seldom important". Rather than just reacting to urgent situations, it is useful to stand back and

If this is urgent, then we must be important!

Sandra was delighted with her job in the training department of a large insurance company. As soon as she joined, she started hearing stories about how busy the department was. Sandra was puzzled as the department was considerably less busy than her previous workplace. Whenever she ventured this opinion, she would be told to 'just wait' and see how busy things got. Sandra found the emphasis on busyness intriguing. Much of the talk was about how busy things were, how late people were working or who had worked over the weekend. She was also intrigued by how badly organised the dept was. Sandra regularly made suggestions about reducing the daily workload through clever use of technology. She would be told that everybody was 'too busy' to set these systems up. Sandra recognised that the department was addicted to urgency. The team saw urgency as a measure of their importance and they weren't going to let anything or anybody diminish that!

identify why a particular issue has become urgent, for example:

→ Lack of planning - something was done badly or important steps were left out and tasks had to be re-done/fixed.

→ Poor communication – not all of the people who needed to know were told or consulted with resulting delays, misunderstandings and bad feelings.

→ The person requesting the work does not actually know when it is needed or does not have a system for keeping tabs on work that they have asked other people to do. They impose an urgent deadline as they want the reassurance of knowing that you have delivered. Weeks later, you might ask about the work you submitted, only to hear "I'm so busy, I haven't even got around to looking at it".

→ Power trip or image management (urgency is the prerogative of important people).

Your Issues

Look through your time log and identify when you were working on urgent items and why. Did the urgency add value, i.e. were you capitalising on an energy and momentum or did the urgency detract from value, i.e. were you re-doing or fixing something that had gone wrong?

Your two key hours at work and how to make the most of them

Your two key hours in the day are your first hour and your last hour at work. Using these two hours effectively ensures that you use your time most productively during the day. The last hour sets you up to use the first hour most effectively.

The Last Hour

Often at the end of the day we run out of time, energy, or both. Sometimes we spend the last few hours of the day rushing to meet a deadline and we leave work exhausted, or we find that we are trying to work on something but are simply too tired so we go home. One of the key factors in really taking control of your time is to use your last hour effectively, to clear today away and set up tomorrow so that you can roll-out as much work as possible.

One of the key factors in really taking control of your time is to use your last hour effectively, to clear today away and set up tomorrow so that you can roll-out as much work as possible.

Here is a great routine to finish the day, and set up success for the next day.

→ Write your to-do list for the following day. Cluster small tasks together

→ Take out your diary and schedule in your tasks in 60 – 90 minute chunks. Start with the bigger, more important tasks then fit clusters of smaller tasks around these

→ Prepare for all the meetings you have tomorrow. Print out documents and make sure your paperwork is in order so that tomorrow you just pick up your file and go to the meeting

→ Check your inbox and voicemail and deal with small and urgent tasks, particularly tasks that other people are waiting for such as authorising, checking and proof-reading

→ Look ahead in your diary and chase things that you need for your work tomorrow or in the next few days

→ Make arrangements e.g. book meeting rooms

→ Talk to key people – your assistant, boss, key colleagues. If appropriate, check whether there is anything they need from

> you before mid-morning tomorrow
>
> → Tidy your desk and put away any files and papers you have been using
>
> → Select an important task on which you intend to spend one hour first thing tomorrow morning. Leave it ready on your desk
>
> → Go home!

This evening routine has a number of advantages:

ⓘ It allows your subconscious brain to assimilate tasks and prepare for the next day

ⓘⓘ It helps you switch off for the evening (this sounds counter-intuitive and many people worry that they will spend all evening thinking about work if they make their to-do list before they go home)

ⓘⓘⓘ It helps deliver an hour of uninterrupted time first thing in the morning

The First Hour

The other key hour in your day is your first hour at work. You can really ramp up your productivity by spending your first hour at work on something that would make a big difference to your job but which is not urgent, e.g. some of those tasks that you identified in exercise 4. Time for these tasks will never be simply handed to you, yet they are the tasks that will help you to produce your 'product' more quickly and with better quality. You need to create and protect time for these tasks.

The first hour is ideal for this important, non-urgent work, for a number of reasons:

→ Many people experience higher energy levels in their first few hours at work

→ There are fewer interruptions in the first hour at work (everybody else is writing to-do lists and checking emails!)

→ You will catch up on the time that you have spent on these tasks. Think about how much work you get through in the couple of days before your summer holidays. Files that have been lying in your inbox or on your desk for weeks get dealt with (or perhaps binned) very decisively

Most of our deadlines are 'end of' deadlines (e.g. end of day), and we tend to meet our deadlines. It is the important tasks that do not have deadlines that need your attention.

You can really ramp up your productivity by spending your first hour at work on something that would make a big difference to your job but which is not urgent

Like most people, Robert, a translator in a European institution, found it hard to accept that non-urgent tasks (like planning or creating great infrastructure) should be prioritised. Robert and his colleagues were often asked to translate difficult material with very short deadlines. Robert was able to clearly describe the differences between translators who were able to meet the challenge of doing a high quality job quickly, versus those who just about made the grade: the high quality translator had a glossary of terms and could access previous translations which had been properly archived (infrastructure). They were up to date with the institution's work as well as developments within their own country (research). They knew people throughout the organisation who could clarify points and provide background information (network). Robert recognised that, even though it is counterintuitive to spend time on tasks that are not urgent, these are the tasks that result in a high quality job done quickly.

Summary of Chapter 2

→ There are five main reasons why we work hard with low productivity:

- Being interrupted and getting distracted, which makes it harder for us to focus

- Switching tasks – which makes it difficult to build up economies of scale

- Using too many task reminders – which makes it hard to get an accurate picture of what we have to do

- Starting with the smaller tasks – which means that we stick with them for much longer

- Urgency addiction – which means that the deadline, not the importance of the task, gets priority

→ Make use of the two key hours. The last hour of the day is used to set up tomorrow and the first hour of the day is used to do something with long-term importance

→ Time spent on non-urgent tasks often helps us respond more quickly

3

Goal-Setting and Planning

Chapter outline
Goal-Setting and Planning

→ Today's dilemma — what is important?
→ Planning — to be more successful
→ Yearly planning — Performance Management
→ Monthly planning — Goal-Setting and why the devil is in the detail
→ Being clever about SMART goals
→ Weekly planning — and a powerful to-do list
→ Daily planning — getting on with tasks
→ End procrastination now!
→ What type of manager are you?
→ The tail wagging the dog?

Too Busy to Plan

Laura had been promoted to the position of fundraiser for a children's hospital and Christmas was her busiest time. Laura had huge passion and commitment for her work but she threw herself into it so fully that she found it hard to step back and plan. This meant that sometimes things went wrong and her hard work was not appreciated.

Working with Laura on a busy day in December, I found that she had not set aside time to plan the quarterly meeting with her boss; not taken time to initiate a key fund-raising project aimed at harnessing people's New Year's resolutions; not taken the time to sit down and reflect on who, in an organisation which counted on many committed and experienced volunteers, could help her to get over a seemingly impossible workload.

However, she had scheduled time to meet with a long-serving staff member to give feedback about a service which she felt was not valuable. Laura had no responsibility for this service. The meeting was not urgent — the service would certainly not be changed before Christmas. She had not had time to think about how to give her feedback or whether this would impact on her relationship with her colleague. Laura was not able to accept that this meeting should be put on hold for a couple of weeks — if it should take place at all.

Laura's story is not unusual. She is simply too busy to plan. But being able to diagnose Laura's problem does not mean you can always identify when it happens to you. From time to time, most of us find ourselves running helplessly in that hamster wheel of activity that keeps on turning — while we stay in the same place.

Today's Dilemma — what is important?

With technology and shifting work patterns executives today **never** finish their work. The internet always provides more opportunities for research. The email continues to deliver cc'd emails about countless projects and initiatives. Executives, whose responsibilities years ago would have merited them a private office and a personal secretary, now find themselves in a busy open-plan office or 'hot-desking' with only a laptop for company. Things move ever faster as time is sliced more finely.

Effective executives realise that quality decision-making is at the heart of good time management. A goal is a choice or decision about something that is important to achieve; something that we want to strive for, change for the better, challenge ourselves to achieve. Setting goals is useful as they give us:

→ CLARITY — we know exactly what we have to do, to what standard, and by when

→ FOCUS - we know what we should concentrate our energy on

→ MOTIVATION — research shows that people who are asked to 'do the best you can' typically do not produce as much as people working to a specific goal

At work, goals come through a variety of channels:

→ The formal performance management system where performance goals are set for the coming year

→ Decisions taken higher up, by the board/senior management/ boss, which need to be actioned

→ Emerging situations, either inside or outside the organisation, which require a response

→ Personal goals that you want to achieve to make your department or team run more smoothly (often to do with areas under your direct control e.g. infrastructure, team members training). Your boss may or may not be aware of these goals but they generally make a big difference and free up a lot of time when they are accomplished

The performance management system is valuable in lots of ways — it forces us to be strategic and look at longer-term business needs, to set goals and look at personal development. Goals are set around important issues which will make a difference — a change of direction, new areas of work, higher quality. Back at work, however, the busyness of the day-to-day can take over and many executives lose sight of these goals.

The solution seems counter-intuitive — spend more time goal-setting and planning. Goal-setting means deciding **what** to achieve. Planning means **how** you intend to achieve the goal. It makes a lot of sense to harness the perspective and energy that goals give us by setting aside time at the end of every month to set goals and then plan how to achieve them. Planning should also take place at the end of the week and at the end of the day.

Planning — to be more successful

It is impossible to specify exactly how much time is saved by planning. what is sure is that it saves at least twice as much time as it takes — and, most likely, considerably more. Most people have painful examples of undertaking seemingly straightforward tasks (like painting a room) and then discovering through experience just how valuable planning is.

When we are under pressure our stress response kicks in. The stress response is designed to make us physically stronger. It's great for running or fighting! But not good for complex decision-making. In order to make the most of your time, regular planning times need to be set aside. And just as business planning comes at the end of the year in preparation for next year, so time planning should come 'at the end of' one period in time for the next.

Yearly	Plan towards the end of the year (performance management, strategy, forecasting, etc)
Monthly	Plan on the last Friday of the month for next month (60 – 90 minutes)
Weekly	Plan on Friday afternoon, for the following week (30 minutes)
Daily	Plan for tomorrow before you go home (15 minutes)

Yearly Planning — Performance Management

Most organisations engage in a number of end-of-year planning activities including developing strategy, forecasting, budgeting and performance management.

Monthly Planning — Goal-Setting and why the devil is in the detail

Here is a relatively straightforward monthly goal-setting/planning system which works for most people. The idea is that you identify what you want to achieve and plan it in as much detail as possible. Having done this, you then work back through your plan to see what actions you can take up front in order to achieve that goal to the highest quality with the least effort. Depending on the complexity of your goals, it should take between 60 and 90 minutes every month.

This can be a useful exercise to share with your team or anybody else with whom you have shared goals.

① Take a sheet of A4 paper. **Brainstorm your goals**, personal and professional, long and short-term, simple and complex. Don't stop to reflect or edit as you write. Write down everything that comes to mind. Allow five minutes for this. Afterwards, look through your performance management document and any other appropriate documents (eg Board or senior management decisions) to check that you have taken account of everything that is important.

② **Choose three of the goals for which you have energy.** Your energy for something might come from an impending deadline, from your boss putting pressure on you, from knowing that something, once completed, will make a big difference. It may be a good idea to choose at least one goal that can be achieved within the month. Adjust the number of goals you choose according to the demands on you and your time. Three goals are manageable. If your goals are more straightforward, you may be able to manage five at a time. Avoid the 'in this place, everything is urgent and everything is important' trap. It's generally a sign that people have lost perspective. Allow about five minutes to choose your priority goals.

③ **Specify exactly how you will know if you've achieved your goal.** You may wish to write your goals using the SMART formula. (For more on SMART and on how to write SMART goals, see p38). Allow about five minutes per goal.

Allow about 15 minutes per goal for steps 4 – 6 below. Some goals will be quite straightforward and may need much less planning time. More complex goals may need considerably more planning.

④ Take a separate A4 sheet of paper for each of the goals that you have chosen. **List each of the tasks that you need to undertake in order to achieve this goal.**

Depending on your preference, you could do a mind map or a bullet-point list. It may be useful to start with the big picture tasks and then break these down into more detail, allowing you to cluster similar tasks together. It is important that you go into as much detail as you can **based on what you know to-day.**

You will be listing three kinds of tasks:

ACTION TASKS — all of the things that *you need to do or initiate*

CO-OPERATION TASKS where you need to *consult, work with somebody else, get information*

INACTION TASKS — when *your task will sit on somebody else's desk* for proofreading, authorisation or additional information

⑤ **Number the tasks in the order in which you plan to do them.** Some people have a preference to

37

Being Clever about Smart Goals

Normally, when we set goals, we think about big picture issues: 'Improve customer service' or 'Make more profit from Product A'.

SMART is an acronym used to describe how to take these big picture aspirations and write them in a more useful way, so that they are:

Specific – Rather than 'improve quality', 'meet ISO requirements'

Measurable – How to know when the goal has been achieved. This can be simple where the goal is quantifiable (e.g. sell a certain number of products). Where goals are not quantifiable (for example, improve quality), the measurement may need to be defined: a specification or checklist that would 'show' that quality had been improved, something that can be observed, having something accepted or signed off.

Achievable – You have, or have access to, the resources to achieve the goal. With effort, it is within reach.

Results-oriented – The goal is focussed on a result or output – not an input. 'Read a time management book' is an input goal. You could achieve the goal without changing any behaviour.

Timebound – You know by when this goal needs to be delivered. This could be 'from now on', a regular date (the first Friday of every month) or a specific date – March 18th.

The advantage of SMART goals is that they are powerful and can focus and motivate an organisation, team or individual. For that very reason, executives need to be careful when setting SMART goals for themselves and for their teams.

A SMART goal is, by its nature, reductive. You have taken a big picture idea 'Improve Customer Service' and asked the question 'How will we know if our customer service is improved?'

This generally leads to several suggestions about how improved customer service could be measured, (e.g. the number of complaints, the customer satisfaction survey, the number of sales referrals).

Once a measurement is established it is likely to drive a significant amount of activity, which usually helps achieve the big picture goal, but not always. See page 44 – The Tail Wagging the Dog.

cluster a number of tasks together and to number the clusters. Others may prefer to number each individual task. For some tasks there will be a logical order: task 2 cannot be done until task 1 is completed. For others, no logical order may be apparent. Number them anyway. You are now creating a route map through the tasks, which can be adjusted if necessary.

6 **Decide when you are going to do these tasks** and write them into your diary, working with the level of detail that you are happy with, allocating specific tasks to specific days or a cluster of tasks to a week.

7 Now ask yourself 'Knowing what I know today about this goal, **what initiatives can I take that will help me to get the best possible outcome in the shortest possible time?'** Initiatives might include setting up templates or systems, briefing key people, involving the team.

This system helps you to get a real handle on the size of a goal. Most people underestimate by a factor of 100% how long it takes to achieve a goal. If you have to send out a marketing brochure, writing 'send out 100 marketing brochures' gives the impression that it will not take much time. Thinking that task through and breaking it down into its component parts gives a different sense of how much time is needed: 'update database, circulate suggested names to top team, print out labels, mail-merge, print and sign individual cover letters, pack envelopes'.

By listing all of the tasks, you can notice links between tasks and how these relate both to the people involved (your team, your boss, people you need to get information from) and to your time-scale (holidays, important company dates, busy periods).

The Devil is in the Detail

People are generally good at steps 1 – 3 above. This part is fun, exciting, big-picture and connected with developing our role and achieving success. The enthusiasm can wane from step 4 onwards when the hard work of real planning begins. But much of the value of this exercise is in steps 4 – 7.

Weekly planning – and a powerful to-do list

Weekly planning is straightforward and simple. About 30 minutes on Friday afternoon should be enough time to:

1 Take out your monthly goals/ plans. Put this week's tasks onto your do-do list.

2 Take out your diary and see whether any of the items in your diary (e.g. meetings) require preparation. Put these on your to-do list.

To-Do Lists

A to-do list is normally written quickly in bullet point or mind-map form and added to as further ideas occur. Most of us use to-do lists simply as a way to record our tasks. But you can really boost your time management by turning your to-do list into a tool which helps you to make quality decisions about your time.

President Eisenhower's famous proclamation 'what is important is seldom urgent and what is urgent is seldom important' gives the basis for a to-do list which can help executives constantly faced by too much work, to make quality decisions about where to spend more or less time. Here's how the Eisenhower Matrix works:

Take an A4 sheet. Draw a horizontal line across the centre of the page (but don't start writing just yet).

The above-the-line space is for *all the tasks which are central to your job;* the 'why' of your job. For example:

→ The things you would tell somebody who asked what your job is

→ The product(s) that you 'sell' to your organisation

→ Tasks specified in your job description and discussed at performance management

→ Things that will matter when you go for promotion

→ Goals that come down the management line

→ Anything that helps you to produce what you 'sell' to a higher standard, cheaper or more quickly

These are the kinds of tasks that you identified in exercise 2 on page 7 and exercise 4 on page 8.

For the sake of simplicity, we will call these above-the-line jobs 'Important'.

The below-the-line space is for *all those tasks that are not central to your job,* but that still need to be done - the 'because' of your job. For example:

→ Requests from others for inputs that it is appropriate for you to provide

→ Compliance tasks and systems requirements, audit, legal, financial, health and safety, organisational policies, etc.

→ Daily infrastructure management - organising email, paperwork, updating databases

→ Historical reporting

For the sake of simplicity, we will call these below-the-line jobs 'Not Important'.

Next, add a vertical line down the centre of the page. On the left hand side, you are going to put the deadline driven tasks. On the right hand side, you place the tasks which do not have a deadline.

For the sake of simplicity, we will call these tasks 'urgent' and 'non-urgent'.

End Procrastination Now!

Most people have them. That small but perfectly formed couple of tasks that they would rather do anything but tackle. They try to forget about them, but these tasks sit like a woodpecker at the back of your head, tapping at your brain, stopping you from enjoying your free time or successes at work.

Procrastination wastes huge amounts of energy, but getting on with the tasks is remarkably simple.

There are two reasons why people procrastinate:

❶ The task bores them. They know what is involved but they find more interesting things to do with their time.

❷ The task makes them uncomfortable. This could be to do with a perceived lack of personal skills or a belief that doing this task may bring them into conflict with somebody. They find safer things to do with their time.

The solution to both types of procrastination is the same:

→ On day 1, set 15 minutes aside to plan the task. Just as you do in step 4 of monthly planning, detail exactly what is involved in achieving this task, based on what you know today.

→ Take two coloured highlighters. With the first colour, highlight all of the tasks that you feel able to do. With the second colour, highlight all of the tasks that you feel unable to do.

→ Working on the second cluster of tasks, write down exactly what help you need in order to tackle these tasks, e.g. advice or training. Initiate communication to get help.

→ Finally, circle the tasks that you are going to tackle tomorrow and set aside some time for these. If you wish, choose the easiest tasks. It doesn't matter just as long as you get started.

→ On day 2, action the tasks that you highlighted yesterday and circle 3 more that you intend to do the next day, and so on.

→ At some stage (most likely early on) you will find that you no longer dread this task. If the task is complex, run it through the monthly planning procedure. If it is simple, incorporate it straight into your weekly planning.

You now have four types of task which you can plot on the Eisenhower Matrix:

Type 1	Type 2
Important and urgent tasks	Important and not urgent tasks

Type 3	Type 4
Not Important and Urgent tasks	Not Important and Not Urgent tasks

Type 1 Tasks:
Important and Urgent

The 'product' that you sell to your organisation, which needs to be delivered on time and to the right quality, including services to clients (both internal and external), reports, presentations, sales. Probably your answers to Exercise 2 on page 7 'My job'.

Type 2 Tasks:
Important and Not Urgent

Tasks that improve the quality and speed with which you can deliver your Type 1 tasks: research, people management, creating good infrastructure, networking and communication. Probably the tasks you identified in Exercise 4 on page 8 'If Only'.

Type 3 Tasks:
Not Important and Urgent

Tasks for other people (including other peoples' goals), administration, arrangements, historical reports, all audit and checking procedures, many routines, compliance, daily infrastructure management.

Type 4 Tasks:
Not Important and Not Urgent

The tasks that are mostly a waste of time. We rarely plan for these, although a few creep in from time to time for historical, political or relationship reasons.

A typical response to using the Eisenhower matrix as a to-do list is 'it will take me more time than the way I normally do it'. That, of course, is its value. Using this list forces you to think about what is important and deserving of more time and what is not important and therefore deserves less time.

This to-do list can be used both for weekly planning (on Friday afternoon) and for daily planning (at the end of the day).

Daily Planning — getting on with tasks

As suggested in Chapter 2 — Managing Your Productivity, you should be taking some time at the end of the day to set up tomorrow. And doing up tomorrow's to-do list is a key part of this.

❶ Take out your diary, your weekly to-do list and today's to-do list. Make up a new Eisenhower matrix for tomorrow.

❷ Take out your diary and plan when you are going to do these tasks. Using 60-90 minute chunks of time, plan the important tasks first and cluster smaller tasks around them.

Having identified what is important, you now need to find a way to achieve your goals — and to complete all of the other work that is not goal-related too.

That's where chapter 4 can help!

What type of manager are you?

The Eisenhower Matrix is a useful model for a to-do list. But it can also very usefully describe your own approach to work. What type of manager are you?

Type 1 Managers (Important and Urgent) tend to meet their deadlines. They rarely have time to capitalise on their work by putting long-term structures in place so they often spend time re-inventing the wheel. This approach can come at a heavy cost to the manager and those around him.

Type 2 Managers (Important and Not Urgent) tend to be pro-active, investing time in systems, research and relationships which help them to meet urgent deadlines quickly and well.

Type 3 Managers (Not Important and Urgent) rush around, get involved in crises, focussing on unimportant issues, staying very busy, continually clearing away the small jobs but rarely getting to the big ones.

Type 4 Managers (Not Important and Not Urgent) spend a good deal of time drinking coffee, chasing rumours, getting involved in things that don't concern them and responding to emails that have been circulated to the whole company. Depending on the organisation they work for, they are either performance managed, sidelined or sacked.

The Tail Wagging the Dog?

Dominic was the manager of the customer service department of a multi-national computer company based in Paris. Along with the seven other members of his team, he worked intense 12 hour days fielding customer queries and fixing problems in what seemed like a never-ending struggle to keep up.

Dominic had no time for management tasks. I suggested to him that he take one member of the team (perhaps himself) off the front line, to log the calls that were made, analyse the problems and then fix the problem which would free up most time for the team. Then, to fix the second most time-consuming set of problems, and so on.

Dominic informed me that this was not possible "because of our goals".

It turned out that Dominic's team had the following goal:

→ 'To achieve a 70% customer satisfaction rating (CSR) on services to clients'. (This was measured by sending out a response card to clients the team had serviced).

The team was barely meeting this goal and Dominic was afraid that if he took one person off the front-line their CSR would go down. Despite the risks of his 'all hands on deck' strategy — which included sick days, burn-out and customers who, long term, were not satisfied, Dominic felt unable to take action which would have made a real difference in the long-term.

Dominic's goal met all the SMART criteria. Where Dominic went wrong was that he was sticking to the letter of the goal, rather than trying to meet the spirit of the goal, which was to improve customer service.

Summary of Chapter 3

→ Time spent planning means a better, quicker job

→ Harness the clarity, focus and motivation of well-written goals

→ Focus on the spirit of the goal, not just the letter

→ Build monthly, weekly and daily planning into your work life

→ Use the Eisenhower Matrix to make the best decisions about your time

→ Distinguish between the 'why' and the 'because' of your job.

4

Managing Your Schedule

Chapter outline
Managing Your Schedule

→ Seven more ways to get the most from your day
  - Batch similar tasks together and do them in one go
  - Plan meeting times carefully
  - Give yourself time challenges
  - Don't be a perfectionist
  - KISS — Keep it Short and Simple
  - Distinguish between tomato sauce and porridge jobs
  - 'Red Line' your finishing time
→ A timetable for quicker decisions

Much of this book has emphasised the importance of quality decision-making. But decision-making is a costly activity, that takes time and energy.

So finding ways to make good decisions quickly is a clever thing to do. The questions below may seem strange. But take the time to answer them.

Q1. Bob is due to make a presentation to the Board this morning. He wants to look good. Last night, he carefully selected the clothes that he would wear:

Vest	Underpants	Socks (2)	Belt
Shirt	Tie	Cuff Links (2)	
Trousers	Jacket	Shoes (2)	

How long do you think it will take Bob to get dressed?

Q2. Which takes you longer?

    a. Deciding what to wear to a party, or

    b. Putting it on

Q3. Where do you keep your:

    CDs? _____

    Books? _____

    Socks? _____

    Forks? _____

Q4. Back to Bob getting ready for his presentation: There are lots of ways that Bob could get dressed. He could put on his socks first and then his vest, or he could put on his underpants followed by his trousers. Of course, he can't put his shoes or trousers on first.

In how many different ways can Bob get dressed?

Starting with question 4: How many different ways are there for Bob to get dressed? The answer may surprise you. Over 194,000,000 ways to get dressed. (If you don't believe this, see page 95 for details).

Regarding question 1 – how long will it take Bob to get dressed? Most of you will have answered 10 minutes or less. So, how does Bob cut through 194,000,000 decisions (different ways of getting dressed) in 10 minutes (while probably rehearsing his presentation at the same time)? Most likely he has a routine and gets dressed the same way every day. **Good routines save time.**

Regarding question 2. Most people reply that it takes longer to decide what to wear than to put it on. **Often it is the decision-making, not the doing, that takes time.**

Think about people who are involved in truly critical situations. First-aid attendants, airline crew, fire fighters - they all have clear procedures which mean that they can move straight into action, without wasting valuable time thinking about what to do.

Question 3 asked you where you keep various things at home. Most people are good at organising their physical space. A rack for CDs, a shelf for books, a drawer for forks or socks (hopefully not the same drawer). Some people like to organise very finely — CDs in alphabetical order, sports socks separate from work socks.

Others are happier with a looser arrangement, all socks together. Think about how exhausting it would be to live in a house where you didn't have set places for anything. How long it would take you to find things, to put things away. **Having places for things (and times for tasks) cuts down on decision-making and saves mental energy.**

How do you create good routines that can increase your productivity, improve the quality of your work and get you home earlier? And when trying to be goal-focused, how do you find time to do all of those Type 3 (urgent and not important) tasks that often take such a lot of the day?

Good routines save time.

It is the decision-making, not the doing, that takes time.

Having places for things (and times for tasks) cuts down on decision-making and saves mental energy.

49

Go back to the task - switching exercise on page 25. Reflect on what the answers you gave tell you about the decision-making strategies that you use.

It makes sense to create routines around tasks which need to be done – but which risk eating up a lot of your time.

If you have kept a time log, now is a good time to take it out so you'll have some real data for working through the suggestions below.

At the end of this chapter, I suggest you create a timetable, just like you had at school. But instead of subjects like maths, science and history, you are going to fill your timetable with the tasks you need to do in order to be successful at your job; this to include slots for regular meetings and appointments, your key deliverables, your development tasks, all of the daily administration and other calls on your time.

At school, the timetable was inflexible, with 45 or 50 minute slots for each class (except the dreaded double maths). Your timetable is going to be much more flexible with slots for different tasks expanding and contracting as your needs change. However, it will help you to save time by providing anchor places for all of those tasks that you need to do, including those tasks that you often do 'before I forget'. There is an example of a timetable shown in Appendix 2.

Seven more ways to get the most from your day

Like most people, you probably have too much work to fit into a working day, so how do you fit them all in? Parkinson's famous law states that

'Work expands to fit the time available'

The corollary of which is

'Or contracts to fit the time allocated'

Here are seven ways which will help you to create a useful routine that allows you to get through your work more quickly. Remember you plan in order to be more prepared, not to be more rigid. Of course there will always be unplanned tasks that need to be done immediately – but the more you implement good time management practice, the fewer these will be.

❶ Batch similar tasks together and do them in one go

Examples of tasks that can be batched

→ Phone calls and emails. Write down the name of the person that you want to contact and a couple of key words or bullet points. Then do all of your calls or emails together. (By writing down you are actually planning and your sub-conscious mind will go into action and prompt you with further ideas that help avoid having to contact the person twice — the 'I forgot to mention' call or mail)

→ Administrative tasks (such as signing, authorising, checking, proof-reading, making arrangements)

→ Financial tasks (such as invoice preparation or checking, checking budgets, authorising expenses)

As you go through your day, try to work on major tasks or chunks of smaller tasks. Don't get distracted from the chunk you are working on. Use your to-do list to keep track of ideas that occur about other tasks.

2 Plan meeting times carefully

The hour after lunch tends to be a low energy time and it makes sense to schedule short one-to-one meetings at this time. During the morning, defer those 'Have you got a minute?' meetings to 15 minute slots in the hour after lunch. Fill in the time between these meetings (if there is any) with small tasks.

Large meetings tend to drag on and a very clear cut-off point like lunch-time or the close of business often help to focus minds.

Tip for Emails

The biggest time saving by far can be made by batching your email. Most emails are opened four times:

i Firstly they are opened and scanned to ensure that there is nothing too urgent in them

ii Later they are opened and read to ensure understanding

iii Next they are opened and acted upon (replied to/ forwarded)

iv Finally, they are opened to decide whether to delete/file.

Many people find that they spend much of their day working on email — without ever clearing their inbox. They are continually interrupted by a stream of messages, some of which are central to their role, but many of which are not.

Switch your email notification off so that you can really focus on the job you are doing. In the beginning, as you change people's expectations about how you work, you may wish to log on to your email every 60 to 90 minutes. But as you establish a pattern of responding to emails in batches, you may be able to push back your routine, opening your email only two or three times a day.

The time at which you start your meeting can signal the expected finishing time.

❸ Give yourself time challenges

Deadlines are powerful. They focus and motivate us. Harness the power of deadlines by giving yourself time challenges. If you normally tinker with the monthly report for eight hours over a number of days, challenge yourself to do the first draft in two hours. Set aside the time in your diary. Plan what you need and prepare. Close the door, turn off the email and get to work. Work quickly and leave gaps where you don't have enough information. Editing, correcting and completing will come later. The chances are that that you'll get 80% of the report done in the two hours. Later you may need a couple of one-hour sessions to finish it off. Result: About four hours saved per month (that's nearly 6 working days per year!).

❹ Don't be a perfectionist

Do you waste precious hours perfecting things which just need to be 'good enough'? Work out which tasks need to be perfect (very few) and which tasks need to be good enough. Often the last 10% of the job takes as much time as the first 90% - but how much value is added?

❺ KISS - Keep it Short and Simple

You probably know more than anybody else needs to know about your areas of expertise and responsibility. It can be hard to step back and decide what is appropriate to share. Many reports and presentations contain far too much detail. PowerPoint, particularly, lends itself to information overload. A good starting point when preparing a report, presentation or meeting is to start from the top with 'the three main points'. then see if anything of real value has been left out. In presentations and reports, don't be seduced by your own material, work out carefully what the people with whom you are communicating need to know.

❻ Distinguish between tomato sauce and porridge jobs

Some jobs, it makes sense to do quickly — like washing out the saucepan in which you made tomato sauce. If you leave it for later, it will take much longer to wash. Other jobs are better delayed, like soaking your porridge pot and washing it later. Wash it immediately and it will take much longer.

Tomato sauce jobs which should be done sooner include:

→ expenses, invoicing and any other job that involves fiddly little bits of paper that clutter up the place

→ putting things away right after you've used them

→ writing information while it is

still fresh - action plans, notes of meetings

→ things that other people are waiting for

→ tasks that start a chain of events or where you need to get into a pipeline

→ applying for resources which might run out

→ writing down ideas, commitments, plans, deadlines

Porridge jobs which should be done later include:

→ Documents that are very important or complex: draft and leave overnight

→ Documents that will have a wide circulation, where completeness and clarity are really important

→ Anything which has gripped you emotionally — particularly where you feel frustrated or angry. Wait before you phone or write. If it makes you feel better, write a reply then save as a draft

→ Anything that presents as urgent. While it might seem counter-intuitive, at least take a few minutes to plan and examine options before jumping in

❼ 'Red line' your finishing time

When you are planning at the end of the week for next week or at the end of the day for the next day, draw a thick red line in your diary at the time that you intend to go home. This works as a strong visual reminder and helps you to stay focussed. If you need to work longer hours, it can make more sense to arrive early and take advantage of a higher energy curve than to stay late while it gets dark.

If you are working chronically long hours, start by leaving on time at least one day a week and work up to two days as quickly as possible. Monday is best as it gets your week off to a good start and you can catch up later in the week. Tuesday is the second best day to leave on time. Most people leave work on time on Fridays anyway. Why? Because it's Friday and ... well, it's the weekend.

A timetable for quicker decisions

Exercise

So far in this chapter, we have looked at ways in which you can get through your work more quickly. The next step is to design a weekly timetable with anchor times for all of your tasks. As with the other plans we have talked about, the objective is to focus your attention and save time, not to tie you into something rigid.

Taking account of the ideas above, design a timetable which will give you time to do all of your tasks, including the Type 2 tasks that often get postponed.

If your work is largely office

53

based, you might have a timetable where roughly the same types of activities are pencilled in across each day of the week, e.g. Type 2 activities from 9 am – 10 am every morning. If you travel a lot or work on a project basis, you might prefer to allocate days or half-days for different activities - Type 2 tasks on Monday morning, travelling and meetings Tuesday, administration on Wednesday, and so on.

So when you carry out your weekly planning, instead of making every week up from scratch, 'drag and drop' your tasks into their anchor places. Using a timetable also helps you avoid doing things 'before I forget'. The following list may help you to identify areas for which anchor times may be useful:

→ Improving infrastructure

→ Creativity and innovation

→ Planning

→ Reading/research

→ Meetings – long/large

→ Meetings – short/one-to-one

→ Regular deadlines and meetings

→ Email, phone, paperwork

→ Administration and arrangements

→ Selling (cold-calling, service calls, follow-up calls...)

→ Working with team members – delegation, coaching, follow-up

→ Monitoring/checking/ authorising/controlling/ proof-reading

→ Performance management

→ Networking/professional development

→ Updating key people/team meeting

→ Drafting/editing/finalising documents

→ Working on Projects

→ Servicing Committees

Worth the Risk?

A manager in a multi-national with a strong meetings culture is regularly asked to make presentations about projects that he manages, at a variety of internal meetings. In his experience, so many meetings are cancelled or postponed, that he never writes his presentations or reports until the last minute. As soon as a request to present is received, he jots down ideas (headings only) and adds to these as further ideas occur. Only when he is fully sure that the meeting is going ahead does he pull the presentation or report together. The manager feels that so many meetings are cancelled, the risk is worthwhile.

Bottlenecks

What are your bottlenecks? What are the places or the tasks that get blocked so that other things back up behind them? For Dorothy, it's coming home from business trips. "The suitcase and the briefcase remain unpacked for days. At home, things pile up on top of the unpacked suitcase. At work, there's so much other stuff waiting. So the report, the expenses, the undertakings to follow-up on issues are all delayed". So unpacking is Dorothy's bottleneck. Bottlenecks come in all shapes and sizes – filing, starting a job, finishing a job, administrative delays. Mostly they are caused by poor habits and mostly they can be fixed by becoming aware of them and making decisions to get things into the system.

Summary of Chapter 4

→ Good routines – based on sound decision-making – are powerful. They save time and energy and allow you to achieve more in less time

→ Collect and deal with your email in batches - opening dealing with and deleting/ filing emails at each session

→ Batch your 'Not Important, Urgent' tasks so that you get them on and off your desk on a daily basis

→ Make use of natural deadlines to maximise meeting effectiveness. Meetings that tend to run on could start one hour before lunch-time. A couple of short one-to-one meetings are ideal for the hour after lunch

→ Harness the great energy of deadlines by creating your own. Challenge yourself to get your work done in half the time. You probably will!

→ Don't be a perfectionist. Know when good enough is good enough

→ Create a flexible weekly timetable with space for all of your tasks. Use this to fast-forward decisions on when to do what task.

5

Managing Your Environment

Chapter outline
Managing Your Environment

→ Your environment has a massive impact on your productivity

→ Why clutter is such bad news

→ 4 Steps to creating an environment that helps you to achieve your goals

Imagine what it would be like to arrive at work to a clean desk and well-ordered workspace. You walk in. Some plants and personal items make your work space welcoming. It is clean and looks cared for. As you approach your desk, you see the to-do list that you wrote before you went home yesterday, together with some idea of how your time will be allocated today. In the centre of the desk is the file that you're going to work on for an hour this morning.

Your environment has a massive impact on your productivity

The environment *in which* you work has an enormous impact on *how* you work. Your environment is sending you cues all the time that affect your feelings, your thinking and your behaviour. Think how differently you feel and behave when you walk into an airport, a spa, your old school or a house in which you spent a lot of time as a child.

And there are countless psychological experiments that confirm how powerful the environment is. For example people are more likely to drop litter in a dirty street than in a clean street and town planners have long been aware of 'broken window syndrome' where a house or car that looks uncared for will attract the wrong kind of attention.

Consider the millions of pounds spent annually by retailers making sure that the shopping environment they create (the smells, sounds, sights and tastes that you experience as you go through their stores) encourages you to buy more of their products. They put the frequently bought products at the back of the shop so that you have to walk past other products to get to them. Advertisers and marketers, too, work hard to get their message into your environment because they know that it influences your decision-making.

The environment that you work in is constantly sending signals to you and to your colleagues about how to behave. And it is worth making sure that your environment helps you to:

→ make the best possible decisions about what to do with your time

→ stay energised and focussed on what you want to achieve

→ do high-quality work

→ let others know how you work

Why clutter is such bad news

Clutter gets in the way of your clarity and focus:

→ *Clutter is tiring.* Your brain processes everything that is in your field of vision, using up valuable energy.

→ *Clutter makes it hard to decide what's important.* Papers sitting on the desk will attract more attention than papers that are out of sight.

→ *Clutter is time-consuming.* People who work at cluttered desks spend time organising what's on the desk. They move papers around, flick through brochures and make piles.

→ *Clutter is stressful.* It's hard to feel in control when there could be problems lurking among all those papers.

The average employee has 40 hours of work on their desk and probably the same again in their inbox! So, for most people, working through everything is not an option; what's needed is a quick and simple method to clear the clutter.

Most people who work in a clean environment really value it. However, people who work in a cluttered environment often resist the suggestion that this has an impact on their work, and get quite defensive saying things like *"That's just who I am", "It doesn't make any difference to my work"* and *"I know where everything is".*

There are two types of people who DO know where everything is on their desk:

→ The first type have created a horizontal filing system where

everything is well organised and within easy reach.

→ The second type know where everything is because they search through it five times a day!

There are many reasons why people are defensive about clutter. A cluttered desk may send a message that you are an important and busy person. Perhaps the cluttered desk is, subconsciously, a sign of independence; a rebellion against adults who insisted on tidy rooms. But most people don't plan to work at a cluttered desk. The clutter grows because papers arrived more quickly than they could be dealt with.

What does your environment say to you and about you?

Take a look at your whole environment – your desk and other furniture, your chair, your equipment (including lighting), your walls or screens, plants and other decorations. Does it look cared for or neglected? Ask yourself:

→ Does this environment help me or hinder me in achieving my goals?

→ Do I have the best possible infrastructure?

→ How could I change my environment and infrastructure in order to do higher quality work more quickly?

→ What does this environment say about me as a person? If I was hiring myself, and had to make a decision based on the state of the workspace, would I get the job?

How to create a great environment

There are four steps to creating an environment that helps you to achieve more:

1 Create a goal-focussed environment

2 Once-off clearance and sorting of the clutter

3 Sort out your storage systems

4 Clear your paperwork and emails daily

Let's look at these in turn:

1 **Create a goal-focussed environment**

The 'call' of things that are urgent but not important is very loud. Phones ring or flash a light to let us know that there's a message. Emails (many with red exclamation marks) and reminders appear on our computer screen. Mobile phones vibrate. Breathless colleagues look for information immediately! ASAP!, Now! It is hard not to fall into the urgency trap.

Many environments are dominated by urgency. The challenge is to create an environment that helps you prioritise important tasks

So, every month do a brief mind-map overview of your goals. Make this as visual as possible using colour, symbols and diagrams. Make colour copies and display these in key places such as:

→ Somewhere you will see them each time you enter and leave your workspace

→ Somewhere very close to your main working space, e.g. on the wall in front of you or taped to the corner of your desk or meeting table

→ On documents that you use when making decisions about your time – taped to your calendar or year planner, stuck into the front of your diary, on the cover of your notebook

→ In other places that you use regularly – stuck inside your briefcase, taped onto your whiteboard

→ Scanned into your computer and used as your screen-saver and your wall paper

Displaying your goals publicly has a number of advantages. It puts pressure on you to achieve your goals, helps you to stay focussed on what's really important, reminds you of what you should be working on (after distractions and interruptions) and sends a message to boss, colleagues and team members that you have things to get on with. The constant visual prop engraves your goals into your consciousness, making it easier to stay focussed.

❷ Once-off clearance/sorting of the clutter

Your desk and inbox should be working spaces, not storage spaces. Once you clear them out, you will be able to keep them clear. Let's start with the desk.

The first step in clearing your desk is to pick up each item and ask yourself *'Why is this here?'* On your desk, you will probably find that you have four categories of things:

❶ Tools that you need to get your work done e.g. diary, phone, stapler. Also information that you need (e.g. lists, codes, addresses, accounts, expenses forms).

Gather these together and keep to hand. Allocate a space on your desk or a top drawer which is easy to reach. Open a lever arch file for any documents to which you refer regularly or notes that you want to keep. For now, just get the papers off your desk. As you use this folder, you can decide to what degree it needs to be organised.

❷ Files and papers that you intend to work on and you're leaving them on the desk as a reminder.

Here you want to make a detailed list of what needs to be done and get the papers out of sight. Draw 4 colums on a sheet of A4 paper with the following headings: Items No., Description, Action Needed, Date Needed.

Go through the files and papers on your desk one by one and complete the table (see example below). Number each piece of paper or file with a post-it note which sticks out to the side, like a tab.

When this is complete you will have one pile of documents that you can easily access via the numbered tabs. You also have a detailed list of exactly what is in the pile. You put the pile out of sight and keep the list in your time management folder.

Item No.	Description	Action Needed	Date Needed
1	Invoice from Company A	Check against tender	12/3/XX
2	John Smith's Strategy Report	Read and comment	15/3/XX
3	Brochure from Competitor Company	Read/background information	Anytime

Clearing your Backlog

On Friday afternoon, when you are planning for the week ahead, you take this list and schedule the items which are important.

> Don't make the mistake of believing that you have to work through everything that was on your desk and is now on the list. Many of those tasks were left there because you didn't really need to do them in the first place and you don't need to do them now. Or perhaps it may have made sense to do the task at the time but no longer. It may have been somebody's whim or one of those 'nice to do' jobs that you never got around to. The reality of our environment is that things change and tasks that once seemed important are no longer necessary.

(iii) **Items that you don't want to throw away but you don't know where to put them, or whether you'll need them again e.g. expensive brochures, documents you may need in the future, letters from people offering you services which might come in useful some day, gadgets, gifts, freebies, samples...**

Take an A4 box (e.g. an empty photocopy-paper box). Write 'Just in Case File' on the side of it. You have now created a place to hold all of those items that you did not have places for. Put the box under your desk and use it for everything that does not have a home but may be needed someday, or is simply too nice to throw away. It's out of sight and available if you need it.

When the 'Just in Case' file fills up you can either:

→ Go through it systematically and see what needs to be kept, what needs to be done, what needs to be filed and what needs to be thrown out

→ Put a lid on it and label it. Then start another box. Keep the box for one year, then discard

→ Throw it all out

The last option is probably best, but it does not really matter as long as the clutter is out of sight.

(iv) **Personal belongings — photos, plants, postcards, thank you cards — that transform a standard issue desk into your personal workspace.**

Chuck out anything that is faded, dusty or curling, or anything that you do not notice any more. Bring in some new ones. Buy a few plants. You deserve it.

(3) **Sort out your storage systems**

Now you need to sort out your filing. Did you know that 85% of documents filed are never used again? Most likely, they were the documents that you filed 'just in case'.

Most people have two kinds of files:

→ Reference files. These are often kept in a soft cover file hanging in a filing drawer for your use, or your group's use They hold information and keep growing as projects develop. They are not checked or audited. Most important work is stored in these files

→ Record files. These are often filed in a hard-cover lever arch file and kept on a shelf for others to record, check or audit

Filing systems that others need to use should be transparent and follow a logical system. If files are numbered, then your virtual filing (your folders in email) should follow the same numbering system.

For filing that is used solely by you, you can afford to be more flexible. Remember the 80/20 rule — you will use 20% of your files 80% of the time. Keep these 20% to hand — and let less used files migrate to the back of the drawer or shelf.

Use the 'Just in Case' file for anything that you only need to hold on to for a while but which does not need to go into your main filing system, for example:

→ Date-related documents which become obsolete once a date has passed (e.g. training course, seminar, meeting)

→ Drafts which become obsolete once a final version has been agreed (minutes, reports, budgets)

→ Documents and other items that you may want to hold on to for a while — but in the long-term are unlikely to be needed again, like notes and rough work for a presentation, strategy document, report, client proposal

Once a year, go through your filing system and get rid of files that are not used.

④ Clear Your Paperwork and Emails Daily

Here are some good ways to make sure that you stay on top of your work — while the top of your desk stays clutter free:

→ Avoid interruptions by placing an in-tray away from your desk. Establish a set time every day to start, do and get rid of your paperwork

→ Use the TROD system to tear through your paperwork every day:

- **Throw it out** - read information, note what's important and discard. Only file if you have to.

- **Respond immediately** - for tasks that are quick and easy (proof-reading, authorising, providing information) do them immediately and place them in your out tray or file. By getting work back to people quickly you build credibility and good-will.

- **Organise it** - when the task is important and will need more time, take a couple of minutes and plan what you need to do on a post-it note. If there are some quick and easy first steps (e.g. asking for information) take these now. Depending on the urgency, add this task to your monthly, weekly or daily planning. **Never put a task aside until you have got an overview of what is involved.**

- **Delegate it** – prepare to fully brief the person to whom you intend delegating the task and give them as much time as possible to work on the task (more on delegation in chapter 6).

Clearing Your Inbox

Many people work with hundreds of emails piled up in their inbox. Just like clutter on the desk, this is time-consuming, stressful and distracting. It needs to be cleared, but a thorough clear out could take days.

Here is a quick and dirty way to clear out your inbox. You need to set aside about one hour on day one, and then about 15 minutes per day for three weeks.

Day 1

1 Create a 'Just in Case' folder in Outlook.

2 Sort the emails in your inbox by 'subject'. This groups email alphabetically by subject line. Other useful ways to sort large quantities of emails are 'conversation' and 'from'. Sorting by 'attachment' can be useful if you wish to print out a lot of documents or to file emails into appropriate project folders.

3 Where you have a cluster of emails relating to the same issue, leave the most recent email (which probably contains the whole conversation) in your inbox. Pull the others into the 'Just in Case' folder. There is a 99% chance that you have just filed away all of the duplicated emails (but still have access if you ever need them)

4 Delete the emails that it is immediately obvious you do not need.

5 Create folders for the other emails. Creating folders in Outlook is easy, quick, transparent, free and searchable! And you can easily cluster folders together as sub-folders. Move emails into their appropriate folders. You may wish to have folders for 'board and management information', 'interesting emails', 'emails with useful links' as well as folders for various projects, clients, goals, and personal issues.

These 5 steps should get rid of at least 70% of your emails. Now for the other 30%:

Next Three Weeks

Sort your emails by 'from'. On day one, deal with all of the emails from people whose name begins with A or B. You will be actioning some emails, deleting, filing and forwarding others. On day two, deal with the Cs and Ds, and so on. In just 15 minutes per day, you should clear your inbox in less than 3 weeks.

Your Daily Email Routine

→ Avoid interruptions by switching your email notification off and setting aside a couple of times a day to deal with email.

→ Use the TROD system for your emails:

- Throw it out – note contents (or not) and delete

- Respond immediately

- Organise – add something to your to-do list. Then file or flag the email or mark it as 'unread' to make sure that you do not lose sight of it.

- Delegate – forward the email to the most appropriate person together with all of the information that they need.

Being Clever About Email

→ Make the subject line do its work. Very short emails

confirming receipt of items, confirming arrangements or even making arrangements (e.g. asking for a meeting) can be written in the subject line. Many organisations now insist that the subject line gives the heads up on the purpose of the email: for information, for action, for reply.

→ Reflect on whether communicating by email is adding value and/or saving time. Often a conversation is better.

→ If you are replying to an email change the subject line by adding to the end of it when you reply. For example, if somebody sends you an email with the subject line 'draft minutes', the subject line in your reply could read 'draft minutes – comments from (your name)'. This helps speed up retrieval and future file / keep decisions.

→ Do not use 'read receipt' unless it is vital. People get really cheesed off by this.

→ Create a separate inbox for cc'd mail (which is generally sent for information only). You can then check through this box once a day (e.g. before you go home). This leaves your main inbox free for all of the mail sent specifically to you.

→ Explore the tools on your mail programme. Some programmes can turn an email into an electronic task with reminders.

Emails from specific people can be highlighted in colour. Emails with specific key words can be directed into specific folders.

Horses for Courses

John, who received over 100 emails per day, automatically deleted all emails that arrived while he was on 2 weeks leave. His out-of-office reply read *"I am on leave and your email has automatically been deleted. If it is particularly important for me to see this email, please resend it after September 3rd".* On John's return from leave 3 emails were resent. The other 997 mails were never heard of again.

Patricia, who was also worried about the huge number of emails that would face her on her return from annual leave, felt that her company would not support such drastic action. She changed her out-of-office message to read: *"I am on leave until September 3rd. If it is particularly important, please resend your email on September 3rd for my immediate attention. Otherwise, I will deal with your mail as soon as possible".* No emails were resent for her immediate attention.

While email is a highly efficient delivery system, many individuals and organisations are concerned about the culture that has grown up around it. Not least because employees spend huge quantities of their time going through email.

Most users estimate that less than 10% of the mail in their inbox is important and useful.

A great question to ask yourself about email is: "If I had to spend the time going through the information in this email with (the receiver), would I do it?". If the answer is no, the chances are that they don't need the email. Similarly, for emails that you receive, ask yourself that same question. "If (the sender) had to spend time going through this with me, would he?" Much email is sent because it's quick, cheap and easy. Not because it's important.

Bits and Bobs

→ Whiteboards/flipcharts in offices: They are used in the beginning with great gusto but after a couple of months, they look rather sad — covered in old plans and out-of-date notes. If you have one, updating or cleaning it should be part of your Friday afternoon routine. Otherwise, get rid of it.

→ Pending Trays — tend to just fill up and up — and then spill over onto the desk. It is probably better to keep a 'pending list' and let documents stay in their files until needed.

→ Think long-term when you are naming documents on your computer, so that they are easy to retrievc (e.g. contain key words) and to make it easy to make keep/delete decisions (e.g. give a good description of what the document is).

Summary of chapter 5

→ Working in a cluttered environment is tiring, stressful and time-consuming

→ Create a great environment by:

  – Making sure that your goals are visible to you and others

  – Clearing your desk and your inbox

  – Making sure that your filing system helps you to access and put away documents quickly

→ TROD through paperwork and emails daily.

6 Managing Interactions

Chapter outline
Managing Interactions

→ 5 ways to move unscheduled calls and visits along quickly

→ Organising and chairing meetings that get results

→ How not to be the victim of other people's meetings

→ Delegating strategically — not operationally

→ 5 levels of delegation that help avoid nasty surprises

Everybody interacts with other people during their working day. Some of that interaction is formal — the time and subject under discussion is planned. Other interaction is informal — calling into a colleague's office, a phone call from a client or meeting somebody in the corridor or car park. The quality of these interactions, and the time they take, has a huge impact on how effectively you use your time.

There is a huge amount of good material on how to develop and maintain good relationships at work. This chapter presents an overview and some ideas about three of the main ways in which we interact with others at work from a time management perspective:

→ Unscheduled/informal calls and visits

→ Scheduled meetings (whether you are organising/chairing them or participating)

→ Delegating work to others

5 ways to move unscheduled calls and visits along quickly

Clearly, when people call at an inappropriate time, the best thing is to be able to tell them that you are under pressure and see whether you can schedule a meeting for another time. Most people dislike game-playing and appreciate honesty. Where you feel this kind of approach is not possible, or where you need a conversation to move on more quickly, the following techniques may be useful.

ⓘ Your Environment

Make sure that your office environment reflects the busy, goal-focussed person that you are. Keep a copy of your goals and to-do list close to you and visible. Keep a clock, calendar or egg-timer on your desk. They quietly say 'time matters' to visitors.

ⓘⓘ Look Engaged

If you spot somebody coming, (or if somebody knocks on your door) pick up the telephone receiver or a file, as if you were in the middle of something. This generally speeds people up or encourages them to ask whether now is a good time.

ⓘⓘⓘ Use a FEDS

A Front-Ended Disengagement Strategy is really helpful in moving through conversations when you are under pressure. You simply tell your caller that you can see them but that you have 'something' in, say, 10 minutes. This generally speeds the caller up and provides you with an easy way to disengage.

ⓘⓥ Use Verbal signals

At the beginning of the conversation set a 'mini-agenda'. Ask your caller 'What can I do for you?' and make a note of what she needs. As the conversation progresses, use phrases like "I've made a note of that" or "I'll get on to that straightaway" which tend to move the discussion on. If you are getting a blow-by-blow account of a conversation, ask "what was the outcome?" Signal progress through the conversation by using phrases such as "my response to your first point would be" and "about your second point".

Coming towards the end of the conversation, phrases such as "my last question", "one last thing before we finish up" or "let's just summarise what we've agreed" will help conclude the conversation quickly.

ⓥ Use body language

Stand up when a visitor walks in and go over to meet them. Find out what they want before you invite them to sit down. During the conversation, it may be useful to make notes from time to time. Coming to the end of the conversation, close documents that you were using and put them to one side. Get up from your desk and walk over to the other side of your office. Do some small tidying up or put something in the wastepaper basket.

These small movements send out signals that you are moving on to something else. If you genuinely find it hard to get somebody out of your office, make sure to call to them. It is easier to leave somebody else's office. Or find a reason to walk them out of your office — a trip to the coffee-machine or photocopier.

Organising and chairing meetings that get results

Most managers spend between one-third and two-thirds of their time at meetings. The average estimate for time wasted at meetings is 60%. That's six out of 10 meeting hours wasted!

Meetings are ideal where quality discussion and sharing of information will lead to better decisions (either immediately or in the future) or better team-working. Energy is generated, commitment is increased; there is value for money. But badly-run meetings, where long discussions result in little or no action and inertia builds up, incur a huge energy cost as employees get cynical and refer to meetings as 'talking shops'.

There are three steps to organising really good meetings and making them worth the time that, collectively, is spent at them:

ⓘ Thorough preparation before the meeting

ⓘⓘ Assertive management at the meeting

ⓘⓘⓘ Timely follow-up

ⓘⓥ Thorough preparation.

Take the time to prepare your meetings. A good meeting will repay your time investment many times over, will get you good press and will mean that people participate in the right frame of mind. Thorough, on-time, preparation also sends a strong message about how important the meeting is. An agenda circulated 10 minutes before a meeting is due to begin sends a clear message to the participants - 'this is rushed.' So make sure:

→ The right people are at the meeting. They arrive on time and know how long they are expected to stay

→ People are prepared: they have received a useful agenda and preparatory papers

→ Where appropriate, managers have held one-to-one discussions with key people about important issues in advance of the meeting, to avoid lengthy discussions that only involve a few people at the meeting

At this stage, the key document is the agenda, which should be:

→ Worded so that people know exactly what outcome is needed and what contribution is expected

→ Thoroughly thought through so that points are in the right order or grouped logically. An estimate of the time needed for each point has been made

→ Kept to about seven points. If there are more than seven items, cluster similar items together as sub-points under a main agenda point

→ Complete — items cannot be introduced without notice

→ Forward-looking. Consider having space for important items which are not urgent, but which will come onto the agenda in the future. Often meetings focus on the urgent while important long-term issues are postponed time and time again.

Make sure that your agenda starts the work of the meeting before it begins by being worded in a way which is very clear and also gets people thinking. Instead of just writing 'sales' or 'sales figures' on your agenda, reflect on a really great question or statement that would clarify what you are trying to achieve:

'How do we increase sales of Product X by 10% in the UK market?'. Once a question is asked, people start thinking about answers before the meeting.

Where appropriate, managers have held one-to-one discussions with key people about important issues in advance of the meeting, to avoid lengthy discussions that only involve a few people at the meeting.

⓲ Assertive Management of the Meeting

→ At the beginning of the meeting allow a few minutes for people to get coffee and catch up with colleagues.

→ Announce the meeting objective and the finishing time.

→ Manage participation so that everybody with something to say gets a chance to talk but nobody talks too much. Be aware that the person sitting silently may need help to 'break-in' to the meeting. The person sharing their opinion on each and every contribution may need help to contribute more succinctly.

→ Summaries are useful in clarifying and moving the meeting along.

Establishing ground rules for a working group of any kind is a great investment of time. Ground rules generally cover areas such as punctuality, what kind of participation is encouraged and how decisions are made. They emphasise that how people participate in a meeting is important.

First, Set all the Rules

The law firm that David worked for had grown over the years and departments were dotted around various buildings in the city centre. Having signed the lease on a new office building, the partners asked David to head up a working group tasked with the move to the new building, including potentially controversial issues like the allocation of space and car parking. One person from each department joined the working group. "In that position, I reckoned that I was in danger of losing friends" says David "so I didn't even bring the floor plans along to the first meeting. That meeting was completely dedicated to discussing how we would work together, how to make decisions, what to do if we couldn't agree a way forward. It worked incredibly well. Having agreed ground rules allowed everybody to keep the bigger picture in mind and there was much more 'give' in the group than I'd expected".

→ The Chairperson or an appointed person keeps a note of agreed actions and decisions – or minutes may be taken. An action list simply notes the agenda point, decisions taken, actions agreed, who should carry out the action and by when.

Actions speak louder than words

Jane works for a multi-national pharmaceutical company. She used to carefully record her department's meetings and circulate the minutes. She began to suspect that nobody was reading her minutes. One day she circulated the minutes in a password-protected document. Nobody asked for the password! She now circulates an action list.

→ Create an action list template and write in all of the agenda points in a column on the left. As decisions are made, write them into the empty column on the right. This helps you in three ways:

- At the end of the meeting, quickly read the decisions or agreed actions back to the meeting. It is amazing how the same people, hearing the same words at the same meeting can all have a different understanding of what was agreed. It is better to clarify now than send out action lists that may confuse people.

- It makes typing up the action list very quick.

- It ensures that the necessary decisions are made for each point. Often meetings jump from one point to another and afterwards it is realised that important decisions were not taken.

Timely Follow-up

→ The 24 hours after the meeting are crucial in terms of maintaining the energy of the meeting and ensuring that agreed actions are carried out so that the next meeting can progress the situation further. The action list should be sent out to meeting participants within 24 hours.

→ If there is a tendency for people not to complete agreed tasks, it can be useful to go through the action list at the beginning of the next meeting, and check whether agreed actions have been undertaken. If meeting participants begin to explain or go into detail on their action points, explain that you are just getting an overview and want a simple 'yes' or 'no' for the moment. Again this sets a businesslike tone for the meeting as most participants will want to say 'yes' rather than 'no' when asked whether they have completed their tasks.

Just a Minute?

Most organisations no longer prepare minutes, for many of the following reasons:

→ The attention of one person at the meeting is compromised by having to write minutes

→ The power of the pen — the person writing the minutes may slant them a particular way — which can lead to long discussions at the next meeting as people explain, defend, challenge what is in the minutes...

→ Minutes record history, what was done and who said what. Many organisations prefer the future focus of the action/decision list.

→ If your organisation still uses minutes, suggest that a decision-list be appended to the front (or is even sent out in advance of the minutes).

→ If minutes are needed, make them as short and general as possible. 'Document A was tabled. Discussion on Item B took place. Decision C was made'. Try to stay away from the detail of who said what as this often eats up time and can also make it difficult for people to shift their position on an issue.

How not to be a victim at other people's meetings

Probably many of the meetings that you attend are organised by somebody else. Hopefully, many of these are well run. But sometimes you might find yourself sitting helplessly at badly managed meetings where the Chairperson is not picking up on the boredom or disengagement signals which are so patently obvious.

It is difficult to fix somebody else's meeting, however you can influence it. Before the meeting:

→ Make sure that your communications about the meeting are businesslike and timely. This sends a message about how you value your time (and people's behaviour is partly about the expectations that you set)

→ If the agenda does not give enough information, ring and ask for it. It may be particularly important to understand the overall objective of the meeting and the objective of individual agenda points

→ Ring and ask if you are not sure why you have been invited and how you are expected to contribute

→ Reflect on whether you need to be there for the whole meeting, or for some agenda points only

→ Ask for the finishing time

Many people sit at meetings where the quality of the discussion is low. Your role as a participant is delicate. You are not in charge. But if you are sitting there feeling bored or frustrated, the likelihood is that others are feeling the same and there will be support for tactful interventions which move the meeting along.

For example:

→ Starting the meeting on time *("I have something at x o'clock")*

→ Clarifying the objective of different agenda points *("Am I right in assuming that we are discussing this because we need to...")*

→ Keeping the conversation on track *("I'm not sure how this discussion relates to the agenda point")*

→ Sharing the conversation around *("I am interested in hearing what XX thinks")*

→ Summarising with a view to moving on *("Chairman am I right in thinking that we have agreed to A and B. Is there anything else we need to do on this point?")*

After the meeting, build credibility by completing your action tasks quickly and letting the Chairperson know the outcome.

Delegating strategically not operationally

John has just arrived back in the office after a three-day conference. Sally, his PA, comes up and announces that the new photocopier has been delivered and that the salesman is waiting to demonstrate it. "New photocopier?" John queries. Sally stops. "Yes, when we spoke about the photocopier the other day you asked me to do something about it. So I spoke to everybody in the department about what they wanted and ordered the best model". "Oh dear" thinks John "I just wanted her to get information. Now what do I do?"

Delegating, achieving results through other people, is at the heart of the management relationship. It's not just about getting people to do particular jobs. It's about the manager strategically looking at the long-term success of his team, the current demands and deliverables and the strengths and aspirations of individual team members.

Delegation is a complex issue, but most managers do not devote enough time to it, resulting in frustration on the parts of both the manager and the employee, loss of time and quality and a damaged relationship.

There are two main issues involved in delegation - time and trust:

→ Time: Does the manager have the time to delegate the work properly, to explain, train, monitor? Does the employee have the time to take on the job? Much delegation is rushed, and incomplete and therefore runs into problems. Time is often used as an excuse for not delegating when the real reason is trust.

→ Trust: Does the manager trust himself enough to explain the job correctly, feel that it is OK to pass the job on, put the right controls in place and then let the job go? Does the manager trust the employee enough to do the job to the right standard, check back in when needed, take correction? Does the employee trust the manager enough to give direction, delegate appropriately and not micromanage?

When to delegate: If deadlines permit, planning delegation should take place when the manager is planning for the next week.

What to delegate: Managers need to be reflective about what tasks they delegate — the essential question for managers is 'what value do I add by doing this as opposed to managing it?' Tasks that are ideal for delegation include:

→ Regular tasks

→ Any task that the manager particularly likes doing and might be holding onto for that reason

77

→ Any task for which there is a structured process or standard way of doing the task

→ A task that someone on your team could do better than you

→ A task that someone on your team could learn from doing

5 levels of delegation that help avoid nasty surprises

Managers need to communicate really clearly exactly what they are delegating at each stage, for example:

1. Gather information and then bring it to me for deciding next steps

2. Gather information. Then you work on that information (recommendation, shortlist, draft) and submit for correction/approval and deciding next steps

3. Gather and work on information. Move to next steps and keep me informed

4. Gather and work on information. Move to next steps and report to me on an exceptional basis (i.e. only if something goes wrong)

5. You are responsible for this. Let me know when it is finished.

To whom should you delegate?

Consider the members of your team in terms of their ability (knowledge and skills) and willingness (motivation and self-belief) to undertake the task versus the time available and the result that you want.

The Final Question

A useful thing to do once you have delegated is to ask your team member to feed back their understanding of what they have been asked to do. This should help to clarify any gaps in understanding. Always agree next steps, sign-off procedures and when the employee should report back to you. That way, you should not end up with a photocopier when all you wanted was a few brochures!

Afterwards, evaluate the delegated task in terms of its learning value for the employee and give feedback about how they did.

Travelling light with a heavy heart

Based in Dublin, Mary travelled at least once a week, mostly within Europe, but occasionally further afield. Over time, Mary grew to hate travelling. She particularly hated airports and made great efforts to spend as little time as possible in them: arriving at the airport just in time, travelling with hand-luggage only (her record was two weeks in China with only hand luggage!) and always reserving an aisle seat at the front of the plane so that she could be first off. With no room to pack gym clothes or a swimsuit, Mary could not enjoy the facilities of the hotels she stayed in. Although hotels rooms were a second home to her, she had no home comforts. With no comfortable clothes to change into, she rarely went out after work.

After a while, Mary saw that she needed to make a decision — change the job or accept the travel. She decided to accept the travel and bought a bigger suitcase — one that must be checked in. She now packs some gym clothes, comfortable 'off-duty' clothes, slippers, some scented oil and a burner. She gets to the airport in plenty of time, and checks in her suitcase. She catches up on reading while waiting to board the plane, taking a window seat which allows her to work undisturbed. She reads while waiting for her suitcase — which usually takes less than 15 minutes. According to Mary "I spend a bit more time at the airport than before, but the quality of my travelling life is much better. I'm far less stressed about travelling and get more work done".

Take the Train

Most people nowadays travel for work. When travelling times of about 4 hours or less are involved, many people prefer to drive themselves, claiming that this is quicker than taking the train (or plane). Thus they will spend a full day driving to, attending and then driving home from a meeting.

While their total time away may be less than if they took the train, the only productive time that they have (aside, say, from listening to an audio tape in the car) is while at the meeting. If they took a train for the same journey, they would probably have about eight hours of productive time, in addition to the time spent at the meeting.

Travelling by plane

Most people go into a state of suspended animation in the airport. It is very straightforward to get a plane: the instructions are printed on your boarding pass. However, with crowds, queues, announcements and checks, it is hard either to relax or to concentrate. Time-wise, you are in no-man's land.

The times in the departure lounge and at the baggage carousel can be useful for catching up with non-essential reading. Non-essential as you need to be alert to announcements, etc. But the time on the plane provides an opportunity for undisturbed, concentrated work.

If you want to work on the plane, get down to the departure lounge early and sit close to where you will board. Always reserve a window seat where you are less likely to be disturbed. Don't sit in the front row (as there are no seat pockets) and avoid the emergency exit rows if you need your briefcase to hand.

Board early and get organised before take-off, using the seat pocket in front of you. As soon as you take off, start your work. Psychologically, you are more likely to have energy for working on your trip out, so make the most of this time.

On the trip home, you are more likely to be tired and may prefer to concentrate on easier things like enjoyable reading material. If you do need to work on the trip back but feel tired, write a plan for what you want to achieve while you travel. Get onto the plane early and belt yourself in. Close your eyes for the 20 minutes or so that it takes to load the plane as this will lift your energy for the rest of the journey.

> If you want to work on the plane, get down to the departure lounge early and sit close to where you will board. Always reserve a window seat where you are less likely to be disturbed.

Summary of Chapter 6

→ Be prepared to move conversations along more quickly

→ A good agenda sends a powerful message — come prepared!

→ Do everybody, including yourself, a favour by preparing your meetings properly

→ Delegation is at the heart of the management relationship and trust is at the heart of delegation

→ Delegation should be used strategically to the benefit of the manager, the employee and the organisation

Managing Stress

7

Chapter outline
Managing Stress

→ What is Stress?

→ The four 'causes' of stress?

→ The stress crossroads — four potential responses to all stressful situations:
  - Do Nothing
  - Change the Situation
  - Short-Term Coping Strategies
  - Long-Term Coping Strategies

→ Worry

→ Relationships

→ The Environment

What is Stress?

Stress is a personal response to something in our environment that we feel unable to cope with. For most people, that certainly includes too much work and not enough time. Trying to cope with vast quantities of information, working across time-lines, meeting expectations about performance, keeping up with new ways of communicating, working in areas that are ever more strictly regulated – these and other issues often leave people feeling overwhelmed and out of control.

There is a huge body of research into stress and the statistics and findings hit the newspapers with frightening regularity – 70% of visits to the doctor that are stress-related, the close link between stress and our physical and mental well-being, the impact of stress on decision-making, relationships and quality of work.

This chapter attempts to look at stress through the time management lens to see how the ideas presented in other chapters can help. It may be that, coming to this chapter, you have taken a couple of ideas on board and are already reaping the benefits of better planning, greater clarity and more focus.

One idea that people often find hard to accept is that their stress is actually caused by themselves. It's a difficult concept. Somebody is rude to me or a delayed plane will mean that I'm going to be late for an important meeting. But it's my own fault that I'm feeling stressed!

It is a difficult concept – but a useful one nonetheless. And, strangely, the realisation about how much control we have over our stress levels often dawns when things get really bad. For example, a person you know may have a very difficult relationship with somebody important, either at work or outside work. Time and time again they complain about this person's unreasonable behaviour and tell you how stressed it makes them. Then one day you ask about the relationship, only to hear, "You know, I just decided not to get stressed about it any more". The same person is behaving in the same unreasonable way. What has changed is the response.- and that has made all the difference.

And once we realise just how much choice we have, we can begin to respond in a more useful way and create a new pattern, a new and more useful habit. So this last Chapter of the book brings us neatly back to Chapter 1 – where we looked at how important our attitude and thinking patterns are.

It is also useful to put a framework around the main things that 'cause' us stress and to look at the variety of responses that are possible in any stressful situation.

The four 'causes' of stress

People tend to get stressed about four sets of things:

1 Worry — 'pre-living' things that may never happen.

2 Relationships — personality clashes, different priorities. This type of stress can be the most difficult to resolve.

3 Environmental — traffic, noise, delayed airplanes, slow networks...

4 Time — too much to do. The most common cause of stress.

Exercise

1 Write down what causes you stress. Write quickly and intuitively without thinking too much about anything that you write. Do this now before you read on. Then see do your stressors fit the four categories above.

2 Now go through what you've written. Choose the most important causes and examine these in more depth. Try to identify what the real cause of the stress is, relating it back to yourself. For example, are you stressed by somebody's 'rude' behaviour because it says that they don't respect you? Or are you stressed by short deadlines because you can't do the job as perfectly as you'd like (and could be criticised?).

The Stress Crossroads — Four potential responses to all stressful situations

We tend to be creatures of habit, responding to issues in patterned ways so it is useful to recognise that we can respond to stressful situations in different ways. Being able to identify how you are currently responding to issues that you find stressful may help you to identify whether your response is useful or could be improved.

The Stress Crossroads describes four potential ways in which you can respond to stress:

1 Do nothing

This is when something is causing you stress and you just live with it. While this is an option, it is rarely useful, not just because it does not change the situation, but because it exacerbates a feeling of helplessness leading to low self-esteem ("She treats me like that because she knows that I won't stand up to her, which proves that she is right to treat me like that").

2 Change the situation

Find a way to put a block between yourself and what is 'causing' you stress, for example:

→ Change communication methods (e.g. communicating by email instead of face-to-face)

→ Move closer to work to avoid traffic

→ Change reporting structure

84

Avoiding what is causing stress may be useful in the short-term or in a very chronic situation where a reasonable change in behaviour is not anticipated. However, there is little or no learning which can be drawn on in the future.

❸ Short-term Coping strategies

This is a range of strategies that can be used in the moment to cope with stress short-term, e.g.

→ count to 10

→ deep breathing

→ take a brisk walk

→ talk to a friend

→ 'justify' the other person's action ("she is acting like that because...")

These may be useful for coping in the moment, but, again, there is no long-term learning and resilience being built in.

❹ Long-term Coping strategies

Building in stress capacity in anticipation of stressful incidents happening. This means recognising that stress is part and parcel of daily life – and we can choose how we respond to it. Managing time is a key factor in managing stress. Stress is not caused so much by working hard, as by working hard without anything to show for it.

Here are some of the ideas that we have already seen in this book which help cope with stress:

→ Develop some key relationships at work. People that you can trust to be honest, to support you and to hold your best interests at heart.

→ Develop a healthy attitude: A healthy attitude is the body's best defence against stress. The ABCDE exercise on page 19 is particularly useful and can be used in absolutely any stressful situation. Accepting that the only person you have control over is yourself opens up endless possibilities for change.

→ Manage stress from the outside in: Pay attention to your body-language. Smile a lot. Use performance enhancing words and thoughts – even when things are tough. There is always a choice to be positive.

→ Don't Fall into the Urgency Trap. Sometimes urgency adds value. A lot of the time it just gets in the way. Be able to stand back and ask 'how did this become urgent?' and 'how best can I respond?'

→ Gain control over your workload. Get an accurate picture of what is on your desk, in your inbox, what your goals entail, what is involved in that job about which you have been procrastinating.

→ Don't carry things in your head – they become more possible when you have written them down. Your monthly, weekly and daily planning is important in establishing a sense of control.

→ Develop perspective. Work out what is important and needs more time, what is less important and needs less time. Allocate your time on this basis.

→ Create Momentum. Well begun is half done. Get the day off to a good start. No matter what happens you can go home feeling that you have achieved something.

→ End the day well. Establish a routine for finishing off the day. It sends 'nearly time to switch off' messages to the brain.

→ Keep your working hours reasonable. Occasional over-time is fine, but constantly working late will make you less productive. Get out of work on time at least twice a week.

→ Take your breaks: The busier you are, the more you need your breaks. Get away from your desk for at least 20 minutes at lunch-time. Even on your very busiest day. You will find that the break gives you new perspectives and energy.

→ Eat a light healthy lunch that will give you energy for the afternoon. If you can, close your eyes for a few minutes at lunchtime for a short nap or

listen to a relaxation tape. This will shoot up your productivity in the afternoon.

→ Don't make everything up from scratch every day. Develop a time template that helps you cut through your work. Harness the power of good routines.

→ Find ways to get out into the fresh air. Oxygenating your brain helps you to cope with a heavy workload. Find ways to get out of the office. One-to-one meetings could take place over a walk around the block.

→ Limit the amount of caffeine that you consume, particularly if you are under pressure. Caffeine mimics the stress response in the body. If you love good coffee, buy yourself the best machine and the best beans you can afford and drink great coffee at home. Most workplace coffee is mediocre so replace it with water or other healthy alternatives.

→ Make your environment work for you. Work at a clean desk, clear out your inbox every day (or at least by Friday).

→ KISS — Keep your infrastructure and your time management system as simple as possible. Less is more. Only add in layers of organisation if they will save time.

All of the above strategies will help you to deal with the stress caused by having too much to do in too little time. But what of the three other causes of stress that we met on page 85?

While the focus of this book is time management, let's just look at how some of the ideas presented in other parts of this book can help alleviate these kinds of Stress.

Worry

While it is perfectly understandable that we worry about people and things that we care about, it is worth recognising that worry is destructive as we replay negative scenarios again and again in our minds. Use Albert Ellis's ABCDE exercise (see page 19) to take those issues that are important to you and to find more useful ways to think about them.

Get away from your desk for at least 20 minutes at lunch-time. Even on your very busiest day.

Relationships

Take the time to nurture good relationships at work. Use coffee and lunch breaks for getting to know team-members and other colleagues.

When you begin working with people, always establish a feedback channel. Not being able to have honest conversations

about performance is one of the biggest causes of stress in the workplace. So with every new relationship at work - whenever you get a new team-member or colleague, or when you are on a newly-established project group - ask "how will we know whether we are working well together?" or "from time to time let's sit down and have a conversation about how we're working together: what's working well between us and adding value, and what's not working well between us and could be changed". This creates an expectation that the working relationship can be discussed and gives you a useful platform for initiating these conversations.

Learn how to behave assertively. Assertive behaviour is much more than a set of techniques. It springs from a real willingness to communicate, to listen, to respect and to do the best you can for yourself, your colleagues and your organisation. It is very much a Type 2 approach that requires an investment of time in the beginning but saves a lot of time in the end. (See recommended reading).

Make sure to nurture relationships with family and friends. There will probably never be a day when you 'have the time' to invite friends to dinner or go on an outing. However, if you invite the friends, the dinner will happen! Or buy the tickets and you'll organise yourself around going on the outing.

Danny was passionate about his job as Health and Safety Officer in a large firm. He accepted that other colleagues did not see his job as adding value. Indeed, he was aware that he created work for them. But Danny was able to establish good working relationships with most colleagues and got the information that he needed to do his job. All except George. When Danny contributed at a meeting, he noticed that George would often raise his eyebrows and look around at the other attendees as if in amazement at what Danny had said. George constantly made sarcastic remarks about Danny's work, using phrases like "life and death", "top priority" or "emergency situation".

At first, this made Danny really nervous. He worried about contributing at meeting and felt annoyed with himself for trying to please George. One day, after his best efforts at impressing George earned him more sarcastic remarks, he said to himself "I don't know what this guy's problem is. For some reason I annoy him, but that's his problem and not mine". As well as feeling a lot better, Danny's whole demeanour around George changed. He contributed much more confidently at meetings and one day, catching George's raised eyebrows at a meeting asked him directly "do you want to say something George?" George looked startled and said nothing. As Danny started to care less about what George thought, George started treating Danny with more respect. It often happens that way.

The Environment

Work out what part of the stressor is under your control and work on that. For example, if the computer system breaks down, it may not be under your control. Having an up-to-date back-up is. For anything that is outside of your control, Ellis's ABCDE model is useful (as it essentially focuses on the one thing that is always within your control — your thinking!)

Exercise

Take the main time management issues that you identified as causing you stress on page 85 and analyse how you have dealt with these issues up to now. Have you just sat back and done nothing (thereby possibly sending a message that you accept what is happening). Have you used avoidance strategies which have removed you from what caused the stress? If so, was that the best possible response? Or perhaps you've used short-term coping strategies (which can be more or less healthy) but which never really deal with the root cause of the stress. Which long-term strategies have you used up to now? Which others could you use?

While the focus of this book is time management, it is useful to note that once we start making changes in one area of our lives, changes often happen in other areas too. So it may be an idea to go through the other areas that cause you stress and analyse your response up to now. Then stand back and see what happens!

Summary of Chapter 7

→ Stress is a personal response to a situation and it is always possible to change your personal response

→ Having too much to do is one of the most common causes of stress

→ We can build in stress-handling capability by using a variety of techniques including managing our thinking, gaining control over our workload and improving our environment.

Recommended Reading

Back, Ken and Back, Kate. Assertiveness at Work (3rd Edition) (2005), McGraw Publishing Company. ISBN 0-07-711428-0

Covey, Stephen. The Seven Habits of Highly Effective People (1989), Simon & Schuster. ISBN 0-684-85839-8

Forster, Mark. Get Everything Done and Still Have Time to Play (2000), Hodder and Stoughton. ISBN 0-340-74620-3

Forster, Mark. Do It Tomorrow (2006), Hodder and Stoughton. ISBN 0-340-90912-9

Also a great website www.markforster.com

Morgenstern, Julie. Time Management from the Inside Out (2001), Hodder and Stoughton. ISBN 0-340-77138-0

Schwartz, Barry. The Paradox of Choice — why more is less (2004). ISBN 978-0-060005-69-6

Simpfendorfer, Ralph and Hourigan, Martin. Time Manager for MS Outlook (2005), TMI.

Appendices

Appendix I

Your Time Management System
Here is what you need to record:

Year to Month

→ Your performance management form and any other documents that record your yearly or longer term goals. Each month, prioritise three goals and break them down into tasks.

Month to Week

The following four documents are needed when drawing up your to-do list and schedule for the week ahead:

→ Monthly goals - The goals that you are currently working on and which have been broken down into tasks with deadlines, etc.

→ The list of papers and files currently cluttering your desk but which you are going to work through your planning system

→ The list of tasks on which you have been procrastinating but which you are going to work through your planning system

→ Your diary with meetings, deadlines and regular appointments.

Week to Day

Every evening, when drawing up tomorrow's to-do list, you need:

→ Your to-do list for the week

→ Your diary

→ Today's to-do list - Check whether all tasks have been completed or need to be carried over.

Your time management system should be as quick and as simple as possible. Only build in complexity if it helps to save time. It does not matter whether your system is paper-based or computer-based as long as it is accessible where and when you need it, but if it is paper-based, it might be helpful to keep it small and portable.

I suggest that you start with a good quality A4 or A5 size notebook. If you already have a notebook that you use at work, allocate a section at the front for your time management. Use removable coloured tabs to mark the pages that you are currently using (e.g. green tabs on pages for all current goals broken down into tasks). Stick your calendar into the notebook. Then use the back of the notebook for notes taken at meetings, etc. If you use a computer-based calendar, print out your week on an A4 page. This normally has enough room for all of your appointments. At the end of the day, print out tomorrow's schedule and write your planned tasks around your appointments.

Appendix II

TIME	Mon	Tue	Wed	Thurs	Fri
08.00	Type 2 Work — Strategy, planning, development				
09.00	Type 3 Work - E-mail, phone, paper, admin,				
10.00	Type 1 Work - Important and Urgent				
11.00	Meetings				
12.00	Lunch/read/walk				Type2 Meeting
13.00	1:1 and small meetings				Lunch
14.00	Type 3 Work - Open door, e-mail, phone, admin				
15.00	Type 1 Work — Important and Urgent				
16.00	T1 Work — Important and Urgent				
17.00	Planning	Planning	Planning	Planning	Planning

Appendix III

How Buck-Naked Bob becomes Ready-for-Anything Robert in less than 10 minutes

Bob has 13 pieces of clothing to put on. Below are the choices that he can make step-by-step	
vst —vest	blt — belt
u/p — underpants	lcf — left cuff-link
lsk — left sock	rcf — right cuff-link
rsk — right sock	trs — trousers
shr — shirt	lsh — left shoe
tie — tie	rsh — right shoe
jkt — jacket	

Step No.	The choice of clothes that Bob has in this step	No. of choices in this step	Running total of choices	Choice Bob makes
1	vst, u/p,lsk,rsk	4	4	Vest
2	u/p, lsk,rsk,shr	4	16	Shirt
3	u/p,lsk,rsk,tie,lcf,rcf,jkt	7	112	U/p
4	lsk,rsk,tie,lcf,rcf,jkt,trs	7	784	Trousers
5	lsk,rsk,tie,lcf,rcf,jkt,blt	7	5488	Left sock
6	rsk,tie,lcf,rcf,jkt,blt,lsh	7	38416	Right sock
7	tie,lcf,rcf,jkt,blt,lsh,rsh	7	268912	Tie
8	lcf,rcf,jkt,blt,lsh,rsh	6	1,613,472	Left cufflink
9	rcf,jkt,blt,lsh,rsh	5	8,067,350	Right cufflink
10	jkt,blt,lsh,rsh	4	32,269,440	Jacket
11	blt,lsh,rsh	3	96,808,320	Belt
12	lsh,rsh	2	193,616,640	Left shoe
13	rsh	1	193,616,640	Right shoe

Appendix IV

Time Management at Home
The focus of this book has been on time management at work, but most of the principles can be applied in the home.

Start by applying the Eisenhower Matrix to your life: the above the line 'Important' things may include your job, family and close friends, holidays and rest periods, personal development, your home and other assets, special occasions, hobbies. Below the line 'Not Important' things may include all sorts of maintenance tasks like commuting, cleaning, cooking, paying bills, looking after your car, checking your bank balance and re-decorating.

As with work, much of our success lies in the Type 2 activities — we work to live, not the other way around. Here are the 5 categories of Type 2 activities applied to your home and personal life:

→ Relationships: Creating strong relationships with important people in our lives. Spending time with family and friends. Playing your part in the neighbourhood or community.

→ Research and Development: Spending time on personal hobbies and interests — whatever they are for you. Staying abreast of current affairs. Staying healthy.

→ Infrastructure: Creating great infrastructure to minimise time spent on all of those 'home systems' — the clothes system, the food system, the cleaning systems, and so on. Also finding the right people to help: accountant, cleaner or gardener. Teaching children to cook, clean, etc.

→ Planning: Thinking about your own life and what you want to achieve in the long-term and short-term. Setting goals for your personal life. Evaluating how you actually spend your time versus what you want to do.

→ Difficult Projects: Getting on with big things that will make a difference — like laying out your garden, buying new furniture, painting a room, organising a holiday.